Springer
Tokyo
Berlin
Heidelberg
New York
Hong Kong
London
Milan
Paris

04 ws

H. Hirakawa, Y.-H. Kim (Eds.)

Co-design for a New East Asia After the Crisis

Springer

Hitoshi Hirakawa
Professor, Graduate School of Economics
Nagoya University
Furo-cho, Chikusa-ku
Nagoya 464-8601, Japan

Young-Ho Kim
President, Yuhan College
Korea

ISBN 4-431-40126-1 Springer-Verlag Tokyo Berlin Heidelberg New York

This book is published as the second volume of Nagoya Economic Studies.

Library of Congress Cataloging-in-Publication Data

Co-design for a new East Asia after the crisis / H. Hirakawa, Y.-H. Kim (eds).
p. cm.
Papers presented at a symposium hosted by the Economic Research Center of Nagoya University in Feb. 2002.
Includes bibliographical references and index.
ISBN 4-431-40126-1 (alk. paper)
1. East Asia--Economic policy--Case studies. 2. East Asia--Economic conditions--Case studies. 3. Financial crises--East Asia--Case studies. 4. East Asia--Economic integration--Case studies. I. Hirakawa, Hitoshi, 1948- II. Kim, Yong-ho, 1940-

HC460.5.C6 2003
337.5--dc22

2003065714

Printed on acid-free paper

Springer-Verlag is a part of Springer Science+Business Media
springeronline.com

Printing and binding: Nikkei Printing, Japan
SPIN: 10930694

Preface

East Asia enjoyed a role as a growth center of the world economy from the 1960s until the currency and economic crisis of 1997. In 1993, the World Bank issued a report entitled "The East Asian Miracle: Economic Growth and Public Policy," in which the bank expressed its admiration for the region's rapid economic development. However, within only four years the region had fallen prey to the currency and economic crisis that spread outward from Thailand. In the midst of the crisis, many East Asian countries began at long last to cooperate with one another in order to cope with these unprecedented difficulties and to prevent another crisis.

In fact, the East Asian region was an exception throughout the 1990s with respect to regionalism. A surge of regionalism, which began in Europe in the second half of the 1980s, spread to North America and Latin America. However, the Northeast Asian region in particular, consisting of Japan, China (People's Republic of China), and Korea (Republic of Korea), did not participate in any kind of regional economic arrangements. Regional cooperation frameworks were limited to countries belonging to the Association of Southeast Asian Nations (ASEAN) and did not spread to the Northeast Asian region.

The currency and economic crisis was a turning point, however, at which point many East Asian countries realized the necessity of economic cooperation and direct dialogue frameworks within the region and began serious attempts to further regional cooperation. ASEAN+3 meetings were one significant example of regional cooperation. The ASEAN+3 Summit Meeting in 1999 issued a joint cooperation statement for the first time in the history of the ASEAN bloc. The Chiang Mai initiative of currency swap arrangements is also a case in point. It is not possible for any individual country to cope by itself with the volatility and instability associated with a globalizing world economy.

A currency crisis must be seen as an unavoidable systemic risk associated with financial globalization. A certain measure of capital control should be introduced into the international financial system. However, institutionalizing capital control appears almost impossible because of strong opposition by the United States. The IMF is also reluctant to accept moves toward increased capital control. In addition, the main economic regions outside Asia have already tried to stabilize their economies and integrate them further, whereas East Asian countries still have only a weak regional system to prevent another crisis. These conditions should encourage us in East Asia to make a greater effort to foster regional cooperation.

Japan and Singapore signed a free trade agreement (FTA), the "Agreement between Japan and the Republic of Singapore for a New-Age Economic Partnership," in January 2002. Singapore had already signed an FTA with New Zealand and has been negotiating similar arrangements with Chile, Mexico, Canada, the United States, and other countries. Thailand and Korea are also investigating the possibility of setting up FTA arrangements. China has pursued a vigorous policy toward FTAs with ASEAN countries since 2000. At the ASEAN–China summit meeting in Brunei in November 2001 the Chinese and ASEAN leaders agreed to start talks toward concluding an ASEAN–China FTA within 10 years. In January 2002 this prompted Japan to propose to ASEAN a Japanese–ASEAN Comprehensive Economic Partnership. These countries are now aggressively pursuing talks on economic integration, especially within East Asia.

Nonetheless, there is still deep distrust among countries and peoples in East Asia. As talks proceed, this will be one of the main obstacles to making progress in economic cooperation. That we must work to overcome this hurdle is one of the factors behind the decision to publish this book. We hope that similar initiatives will be taken in every country of the region in order to allow open discussion on regional cooperation and create a common view as well as institutionalizing the notion of regional talks. At the same time, East Asian countries and peoples must gain mutual trust through such processes.

All the papers collected in this volume were originally submitted at a symposium held on February 7, 2002, organized by the Economic Research Center of Nagoya University, Japan. The papers were subsequently revised and edited. We would like to thank the speakers at the symposium and authors of this volume: Professor Eisuke Sakakibara of Keio University, Japan; Professor Angang Hu of Tsinghua University, China; Professor Walden Bello of the University of the Philippines; Professor Linfei Song from the Jiangsu Provincial Academy of Social Sciences, China; Dr. Chris Baker from Bangkok and Professor Pasuk Phongpaichit of Chulalongkorn University, Thailand, who presented a jointly written paper. We would also like to acknowledge the help of Dr. J. Thomas Lindblad, Associate Professor at the University of Leiden, the Netherlands, and Dr. Ferdinand C. Maquito, Researcher at Sekiguchi Global Research Association and Adjunct Professor at Temple University Japan, both of whom were foreign research fellows of the Economic Research Center in 2002 and 2003, and who kindly participated in our editing work.

Thanks are also due to the staff of the Economic Research Center and colleagues at the Graduate School of Economics of Nagoya University, as well as the co-sponsor, the Alumni Foundation of the School of Economics at Nagoya University, known as Kitan-kai. We would also like to express our appreciation to the President of Nagoya University, Professor Minoru Matsuo, and Vice President Professor Nobuhiro Okuno. Support was also provided by the *Asahi Shimbun* newspaper, the Tokai Local Finance Bureau, the Ministry of Finance, Japan, and the Nagoya Chamber of Commerce and Industry.

Hitoshi Hirakawa
Young-Ho Kim

Contents

About the Authors

Bello, Walden (b. 1945); obtained his Ph.D. in sociology from Princeton University. He is Professor of Sociology and Public Administration at the University of the Philippines and Executive Director of "Focus on the Global South". He has written many articles that have appeared in international journals and other publications, including the *Review of International Political Economy, Foreign Policy, Le Monde,* and *Development Dialogue*. He is also the author of 12 books on Asian and global economic and political issues, including *The Future in the Balance: Essays on Globalization and Resistance* (Oakland 2001).

Hirakawa, Hitoshi (b. 1948); received his Ph.D. in economics from Kyoto University. He is a professor at the Economic Research Center, Graduate School of Economics, at Nagoya University and a former professor in Asian economies at Tokyo Keizai University, Ibaraki University, and Nagasaki Prefectural University. He is the author of several books on Asian economies and economic history, including *NIEs: World System and Development* (Tokyo 1992; in Japanese), and (with Hiroshi Shimizu) *Japan and Singapore in the World Economy: Japan's Economic Advance into Singapore 1870–1965* (London and New York 1999).

Hu, Angang (b. 1953); received his Ph.D. in engineering at the Chinese Academy of Sciences. He is a professor in the School of Public Policy and Management at Tsinghua University in Beijing. At the time of the symposium, he was a research fellow at the Kennedy School of Government of Harvard University. He has also been a research fellow at the Massachusetts Institute of Technology and the Chinese University of Hong Kong. He has published many papers and books on Chinese studies and human development, including (with Shaoguang Wang) *The Political Economy of Uneven Development: The Case of China* (New York 1999). He also contributed to the UNDP publication *Human Development Report of China, 1999* (Oxford 2000).

Kim, Young-Ho (b. 1940); obtained his Ph.D. in economics from Osaka City University. He is the president of Yuhan College, a research professor at Korea University, and an emeritus professor at Kyung Pook National University. At the time of the symposium he was a professor at Kyung Pook National University in Taegu. He is also a former Minister of Commerce, Industry and Energy, the Republic of Korea. He was also a professor at Osaka City University and the University of Tokyo. He has written numerous articles and books, including *East Asian Industrialization and World Capitalism: The Fourth-Generation Theory of Industrialization* (Tokyo 1988;

in Japanese). He won the Dasan Economics Prize, one of the most prestigious economics awards in Korea.

Phongpaichit, Pasuk (b. 1946); obtained a Ph.D. in economics from the University of Cambridge and is Professor of Economics at Chulalongkorn University in Bangkok. Her co-author **Chris Baker** (b. 1948) is an independent researcher of the Thai economy, living in Bangkok. He received a Ph.D. from the University of Cambridge. They have co-authored several books on recent economic developments in Thailand including *Thailand: Economy and Politics* (Oxford 1995), *Thailand's Boom and Bust* (Chiang Mai 1999), and *Thailand's Crisis* (Chiang Mai 2000).

Sakakibara, Eisuke (b. 1941); obtained his B.A. from the University of Tokyo and a Ph.D. in economics from the University of Michigan. He is a professor at Keio University in Tokyo and is Director of the Global Research Security Center at Keio. He is a former Vice-Minister of Finance for International Affairs in Japan. He has written many books and articles, including "The End of Progressivism" (*Foreign Affairs*, September–October 1995) and "The End of Market Fundamentalism" (mimeograph; speech delivered at the Foreign Correspondents Club of Japan, Tokyo, January 1999).

Song, Linfei (b. 1948); received his B.A. in philosophy from Nanjing University. He is the president of the Jiangsu Provincial Academy of Social Sciences, where he is also a professor, and is a member of the Chinese People's Political Consultative Conference. He is the author of several books, including *The Future of China's "Economic Miracle" and Policy Selection* (1996), and *The Western Sociology Theory* (1997), both in Chinese.

1. Introduction

Hitoshi Hirakawa

This volume contains the proceedings of an international symposium held on February 7, 2002, by the Economic Research Center (ERC) at the Graduate School of Economics of Nagoya University, Nagoya, Japan. It is part of the regular activities of the ERC to host an international conference or symposium each year on a highly relevant theme in economics and economic policy-making. The theme of the 2002 symposium was "Co-design for a New East Asia After the Crisis."

This theme was developed by the ERC symposium organizing committee in collaboration with the co-editor of this volume, Professor Young-Ho Kim, the President of Yuhan College, Republic of Korea (Korea), who was a visiting professor at the ERC the year before the symposium. Professor Kim, who was the first speaker at the symposium, and the organizing committee were of one mind about the importance of creating a common vision of a future East Asia of diversity within a framework of close cooperation. We must deepen trust in the East Asian region through co-designing the future since there is a long history of deep distrust in the region, especially in Northeast Asia (Appendix I).

Before we proceed, the editors would like to draw the readers' attention to one thing. The order of papers in this volume is different from the order of the speakers' presentations at the symposium. Although Kim's presentation was made first at the symposium, his paper has become the last chapter in this volume and Hirakawa's paper, which was the last presentation, has become the first chapter in order to explain the general view of regional cooperation in East Asia after the currency crisis in 1997.We hope that these editorial considerations help readers to understand more easily the present development and problems of East Asian regional cooperation.

The symposium itself consisted of two sessions and a concluding panel discussion (Appendix II). The first session focused on the institutional framework for regional economic cooperation in East Asia, in particular with regard to international trade and finance. This session was chaired by Professor Ryuhei Okumura of Nagoya University and featured presentations from Professor Young-Ho Kim, Professor Eisuke Sakakibara of Keio University, Tokyo, and Professor Angang Hu of Tsinghua University in Beijing. Comments were given by Mr. Hidehito Fujiwara, an editorial writer for the *Asahi Shimbun* newspaper, Professor Junichi Naito of the ERC, and Professor Kazuyoshi Uehara of Kyoto University.

In his presentation "Towards a New Framework of Regional Integration in East Asia," Professor Kim advocated the establishment of a free trade agreement (FTA) in East Asia, embracing Korea, Japan, and China (People's Republic of China), that would have significant impact on the economic development of the whole region. Despite the establishment of the ASEAN Free Trade Area (AFTA), barriers presented by nationalism remain a problem in Northeast Asia, and even in Southeast Asia. Historical misunderstandings still have not been resolved, leading to distrust between related institutions. In Northeast Asia, he pointed out, a direct dialogue is needed, and the establishment of an East Asia FTA promotion council was proposed. One of the conditions for economic integration is freedom from the past, according to Professor Kim. He also presented a unique design for regional integration in East Asia, different from the one in Western Europe.

Professor Sakakibara presented a paper, "East Asia and the Reorientation of the World Economy: Building a Regional Institutional Infrastructure," in which he explored the post-September 11 economic landscape. He argued that September 11 shattered in one day the perception of the invincibility of the world's only superpower. More importantly, however, this dramatic event, in leading to the consequent war on terrorism and a change in the Bush Administration's foreign policy from a unilateral to multilateral focus, may very well be symbolic of the beginning of the end of *Pax Americana*. It may also be a harbinger of a more multilateral and decentralized pattern of world governance, one aspect of which is the apparent reorientation of the world economy from West to East. This new world order is being shaped by a growth in regionalization across the globe and by the recognition, engendered by the East Asian financial crisis, of the imperfection and lack of governance of globalized markets. Professor Sakakibara's paper addresses the issue of the value added to national governments in East Asia by regional institutions, such as ASEAN and the Asia Pacific Economic Cooperation (APEC) forum, versus international organizations, such as the International Monetary Fund (IMF) and the World Trade Organization (WTO). A strong case is presented in favor of the establishment of regional organizations in East Asia, and a strategy for the establishment of regional mechanisms consistent with existing global institutions is proposed.

In his presentation "A Free Trade Agreement Policy for the Northeast Asian Countries and ASEAN: A View from China," Professor Hu demonstrated how a regional FTA would speed up economic and trade integration in Northeast Asia. He cited some relevant statistics: East Asia has one-third of the world's population, it accounts for 27% of the world's total gross domestic product (at purchasing-power parity), 23% of world imports, 26% of world exports. Northeast Asia accounts for 19% of world energy consumption, and 22% of world CO_2 emissions. Total foreign exchange savings in the Northeast Asian region amount to as much as $US615 billion. Yet trade liberalization is slow and domestic market barriers relatively high, limiting the potential for both economic and trade growth and regional integration. A step-by-step procedure is suggested for first establishing an FTA involving China, Japan, Korea, and Hong Kong, then proceeding to cooperation with the AFTA, eventually accepting participants from South Asia and the Pacific.

The second session was devoted to discussion of the prospect for future regional economic integration, both in general and as seen from individual countries. Speakers were Professor Walden Bello from the University of the Philippines and the Executive Director of Focus on the Global South, Professor Linfei Song from the Jiangsu Provincial Academy of Social Sciences, China, Dr. Chris Baker from Bangkok and myself. Dr. Baker, Professor Johzen Takeuchi of Nagoya University, and Associate Professor Suranart Khamanarong of Khon Kaen University in Thailand delivered comments. Professor Makoto Tawada of Nagoya University chaired the session.

The provocative title of Professor Bello's presentation, "Strategic Economic Cooperation or Balkanization," immediately conveys the dilemma facing East Asia at this time. He argues there is no choice but to move toward a higher degree of strategic economic cooperation and integration, but the road toward this goal is full of pitfalls and there has been an alarming lack of direction in recent decades. However, he argued, in order to be successful East Asia must popularize and democratize its attempts at regional cooperation and integration rather than pursue elite projects. Japan must also be free from fear of the United States, whose strategic policy has as its thrust to keep Asia weak politically, economically, and militarily. East Asian countries and peoples are now at the point of becoming either a major player collectively in the global economy, or marginal actors in an economically balkanized part of the world.

In his paper "China's Economic Development and Regional Cooperation in East Asia," Professor Song addressed seven key questions related to problems of economic cooperation among countries in East Asia and suggested some tentative solutions. These questions concern the basic framework for regional cooperation, the appropriate starting point, alternative hosts for coordinating the process, imagined and real political obstacles to cooperation, economic obstacles, the importance of Chinese economic development to regional economic integration, and, finally, ways to enhance intergovernment coordination during the process of integration.

Dr. Chris Baker presented a paper co-written with Professor Pasuk Pongphaichit, titled "Experience and Prospects of Financial Cooperation in ASEAN." Dr. Baker and Professor Pongphaichit argued that financial cooperation is inseparable from broader issues of international relations and geopolitics. Moves toward financial cooperation in ASEAN began only in the 1990s after capital account liberalization had exposed member states to international financial instability. The debate on regional schemes took place between non-ASEAN players. The Chiang Mai Initiative (CMI) for currency swap arrangements pioneered a proto-South–North East Asia region of cooperation. It consisted of a network of bilateral pacts rather than a single centralized scheme. Recent initiatives in trade cooperation have taken a similar direction, and these schemes perhaps indicate a new basis for economic cooperation, which reflects the political and economic realities of the region.

In my own presentation, "Globalization and Regional Cooperation in East Asia," I considered the development of a regional framework of cooperation against the background of the recent currency crisis. At the beginning, the cause of the Asian crisis was sought in the structural weakness of the Asian model of capitalism, especially on the part of the United States and the IMF, which are followers of neoclassical economics. Although at a later stage financial speculation, excess capital liquidity, and/or a self-fulfilling prophecy leading to crisis came to be considered the main causes of the crisis, the United States and the IMF did not accept this interpretation on a fundamental level, and the United States remains strongly opposed to any regulation of international capital flow. This forced Asian countries to pursue regional cooperation. I traced the progress of regional cooperation since the crisis. At long last, trust among East Asians and economic reforms in member countries were confirmed as a natural foundation for successful cooperation. This could create the real possibility for a new East Asian common society or community.

The Nagoya symposium was concluded with a panel discussion on the theme "Co-design for a New East Asia After the Crisis." The panel was chaired by Professor Atsushi Kitahara, Director of the Economic Research Center at Nagoya University, and heard comments from Professor Ryoichi Namikawa and Dr. Shimin Shi of Nagoya University. Only a brief summary of the discussion can be given here.

The panel discussion began with responses to the papers presented earlier in the day. All the speakers and participants agreed on the importance of regional cooperation in East Asia. They also acknowledged that there were many hurdles in the way of successful economic cooperation and such things as free trade agreements and currency stability will be difficult to achieve. The tasks facing East Asians can be broken down into four categories. The first one is the issue of creating mutual trust among East Asian countries and peoples. There is much diversity in this region. The problem of historical antipathy between Japan and other Northeast Asian countries has still not been resolved. Recently, with its growing economic and military power, China has emerged as a threat in East Asia. We must overcome such difficulties through deepening mutual trust. Professor Kim proposed the creation of a variety of forums for direct dialogue, especially among Northeast Asians, at multiple levels of society.

The second challenge is coordination between various countries with a view to fostering regional cooperation. Professor Sakakibara argued persuasively that currency stability requires macroeconomic policy coordination between countries, as the European experience of currency integration has shown. FTAs in East Asia require each country to undertake structural economic reform, according to Professor Kim. He referred to the structural reform effect of FTAs as an important measure, especially for Japan.

In Japan there is strong political pressure against liberalization of trade in agricultural products. Some politicians representing voters with an interest in agricultural production become strong protectionists in order to keep their position. This agricultural protectionism presents an obstacle for the "industrialization of agriculture." Professor Namikawa proposed the internationalization of Japanese agriculture instead of agricultural protectionism.

A number of problems were discussed during the symposium regarding the possible impact of the creation of FTAs on China. As productivity in agriculture in China is rather low, the conclusion of any FTA between China and other countries will necessarily have considerable negative effects on peasant farmers in the country. China has to overcome such problems. Professor Uehara, Professor Ho, Mr. Fujiwara, Professor Takeuchi and others discussed the difficulties that China's agriculture would face after any liberalization of trade in agricultural products. Dr. Baker proposed the necessity of regional resolutions for agricultural problems.

The third point of discussion was the influence of the development of regional cooperation on other areas and possible reactions from these areas. As several speakers pointed out, the United States has remained fundamentally opposed to moves toward regionalism in East Asia because development in this area would inevitably weaken U.S. hegemony in East Asia. Professor Sakakibara, Professor Bello, Dr. Baker, and others debated these issues. They confirmed that moves toward regional cooperation would not mean the exclusion of the United States from the East Asian region, but would give East Asian countries equal status with the United States. In this regard, Professor Bello emphasized the importance of a change in Japanese policy that would shift emphasis away from the relationship with the United States in favor of that with East Asian nations.

The fourth point examined was the question of what kind of society or community a more cooperative East Asia would become. Professor Kim discussed the necessity of creating civil societies in East Asia. Professor Bello also insisted that the participation of NGOs and ordinary people in the process of regional cooperation was essential if East Asia was able to build a society of both equity and diversity. Mr. Fujiwara expressed the opinion that China is now surely changing to a freer society even though its political system is not democratic and the Communist party still predominates. He also expressed the expectation that the Chinese government will proceed with political reforms by itself as a major state in East Asia. China and Japan should both pursue the common interests of East Asia instead of only their own interests as two major economic and political powers in the region.

The chairman, Professor Kitahara, delivered a summary, and he closed the panel discussion. Professor Kitahara summarized by saying that East Asia must work toward strengthening regional cooperation in a globalizing world, the necessity of closer cooperation having been shown by the financial crisis that struck the region. East Asia should increase its capacity for self-coordination within the region through cooperation, and aim to create civil societies with diversity. However, the development of regional economic cooperation, and FTAs in particular, will not only require structural economic reforms in each member country, but will also change the relationship between this and other regions, especially with the United States. While these tasks appear to be very difficult, East Asians must work to overcome the difficulties before them and meet the challenge of creating a stronger, better East Asia.

Appendix I. The Purpose of the International Symposium "Co-design for a New East Asia After the Crisis"

The symposium had two purposes. The first was to confirm the increasing necessity of cooperation between the peoples and countries of East Asia as globalization continues apace. The second purpose was to consider regional cooperation in the true sense of the term and create a co-design for a new East Asia.

East Asia's currency and economic crisis, which started with the Baht crisis in Thailand on July 2, 1997, was a result of the inability of East Asian countries, having grown through exporting manufactured goods, to cope effectively with financial globalization. With this as a turning point, countries and peoples in East Asia consciously began to pursue a regional framework for the first time in their history. Realization of ASEAN+3 meetings is a case in point. While it may be insufficient for each country individually to try to strengthen its real economy to cope with volatility and instability associated with financial globalization, the need for regional cooperation has increased steadily. The crisis made it clear that regional integration had gone further in Europe and in the Americas, in parallel with globalization, than in East Asia. It is safe to say that East Asian countries were late in recognizing the risks associated with globalization, fixated as they were with the hyper-growth of the region.

The Economic Research Center of the Graduate School of Economics of Nagoya University held the 15th international symposium on the "Post-Crisis Asian Economies and their Prospects for Further Reform" in March 2001. At this meeting it was hoped that participants would build on earlier symposiums and make suitable suggestions for further progress in regional cooperation in the fields of economics, currency, and finance, through such means as currency swap treatments, free trade agreements, and an Asian Monetary Fund. Additionally, participants at the symposium were hoping to help to build a framework for mutual understanding among people in East Asia.

The second purpose of the symposium might be described as creating "a common vision" for an East Asia displaying diversity in culture, language, history, and other areas. In doing so, a "process" for realizing a common vision was stressed. This is the reason why the term "co-design" was chosen for the conference and for this book.

On September 11, 2001, the terrorist attacks on the World Trade Center in New York and other American targets and the ensuing Afghan War made a great impact on the straight path of globalization led by the United States. At present, a world order allowing for a level of diversity is needed, and regional cooperation, which goes beyond national borders, must be strengthened further. We hope that the symposium and this book will help to advance the cause of regional cooperation and prosperity and peace in East Asia.

Appendix II. Symposium Program

On February 7, 2002, the Economic Research Center (ERC) of the Graduate School of Economics of Nagoya University held its 16th international symposium at Nagoya University in Nagoya, Japan. The symposium was on "Co-design for a New East Asia After the Crisis." This symposium, organized by the ERC's organizing committee in collaboration with Professor Young-Ho Kim of Kyung Pook National University of Korea, and was jointly sponsored by the Alumni Foundation of the School of Economics of Nagoya University, known in Japanese as Kitan-kai. The symposium included seven papers, with the program listed below, using the speaker's original titles.

February 7, 2002
9:30 a.m. – 9:50 a.m.

Opening Remarks by Nobuhiro Okuno, Professor and Vice President of Nagoya University, Makoto Hosomi, Director-General of the Tokai Local Finance Bureau of the Ministry of Finance, Japan, and Kunihiko Okada, President of the Kitan-kai.

9:50 a.m. – 12:05 p.m. Session I

Chairperson: Ryuhei Okumura, Professor, Nagoya University

Young-Ho Kim, Professor, Kyung Pook National University, and Former Minister of Commerce, Industry and Energy, Korea

"Towards a New Framework for Economic Integration in East Asia"
Comment: Hidehito Fujiwara, Editorialist, *Asahi Shimbun* newspaper, Japan

Eisuke Sakakibara, Professor, Keio University, Japan, and Former Vice-Minister of Finance for International Affairs, Japan

"Regional Cooperation in East Asia: with Special Reference to Financial Cooperation"
Comment: Junichi Naito, Professor, Nagoya University

Angang Hu, Professor, Tsinghua University, China, and Director of the Center for China Studies, Chinese Academy of Sciences, China

"The Free Trade Agreement Policy for Northeast Asian Countries and ASEAN: A View from China"
Comment: Kazuyoshi Uehara, Professor, Kyoto University, Japan

13:20 p.m. – 16: 10 p.m. Session II

Chairperson: Makoto Tawada, Professor, Nagoya University

Walden Bello, Professor, University of the Philippines, The Philippines, and Executive Director of "Focus on the Global South", Bangkok, Thailand

"Globalization and the Prospects for People's Cooperation in East Asia"
Comment: Chris Baker, Independent Researcher, Thailand

Linfei Song, Professor and President, Jiangsu Provincial Academy of Social Sciences, China

"China's Economic Development and Regional Cooperation in East Asia"

Comment: Johzen Takeuchi, Professor, Nagoya University

Chris Baker, Independent Researcher on the Thai Economy, Thailand

"ASEAN: Internal Pressures and External Constraints on Regional Cooperation"

Comment: Khamanarong Suranat, Associate Professor, Khon Kaen University, Thailand

Hitoshi Hirakawa, Professor, Economic Research Center, Nagoya University

"Globalization and Regional Cooperation in East Asia"

16:30 – 18:30 Panel Session

Chairperson: Atsushi Kitahara, Professor, and Director of Economic Research Center, Nagoya University

Panelists: Speakers and Ryoichi Namikawa, Professor, Nagoya University, and Minsei Shi, Associate Professor, Economic Research Center, Nagoya University

18:30

Closing Remarks by Atsushi Kitahara, Professor and Director, Economic Research Center, Nagoya University

2. Globalization and Regional Cooperation in East Asia

Hitoshi Hirakawa

1. Introduction

Since the 1990s, the acceleration of globalization has changed the structure of regional economies and is giving rise to a new world economic framework through intensifying the volatility of world financial flows. The region of East Asia enjoyed economic development as an international center of growth through the first half of the 1990s. However, in the second half of the decade, the region was hit by an economic crisis. Then, seeming to have returned to a growth track for a while, economic activity became sluggish. At present, East Asian countries are embarking to varying extents upon difficult structural reforms. Furthermore, there are additional complicating factors, such as the influence of the terrorist attacks of September 11, 2001, in the United States, and the admission of People's Republic of China (China) to the World Trade Organization (WTO) in November of the same year. Thus, East Asia faces the problem of forming a new international economic and political order in the region.

The currency crisis brought a major transformation to the region. After the crisis, frameworks for regional cooperation in East Asia were created and have since then developed rapidly. Such frameworks will undoubtedly increase East Asia's economic prosperity and the prospects for peace. In the twenty-first century, although the economy of East Asia will be especially influenced by China's development and return to the world economy, its prospects will not be those where countries compete on the basis of their national economy alone. The necessity of a framework for regional cooperation is greater than before.

In fact, globalization tends to be associated with the rise of regionalism. In East Asia, regionalism has spread rapidly, although the trend was rather weak until the middle of the 1990s. The reason for this is the fact that every country in East Asia will be subject to the instabilities associated with globalization unless they strengthen mutual cooperation. Increased cooperation stands a good chance of creating a new, regional society in East Asia during the twenty-first century. Whether we achieve this or not, is our choice.

This chapter considers the background of the development of a regional framework of cooperation with East Asia's currency crisis as a catalyst as well as examining the possible course of future developments.

2. East Asia's Currency Crisis and Its Lessons

2.1 East Asia's Currency Crisis and the Response

The 1990s were a decade when East Asia's economy experienced a fall from the peak of economic growth to the depths of currency crisis. Until the crisis occurred, the "orthodox" view based on neoclassical economics had asserted only the merits of globalization. Yet, the currency crisis, which was initially thought likely to affect only Thailand, turned into a crisis for the entire region, spreading even to Russia, Latin America, and other areas through "contagion," and ending with the near-collapse of a famous American hedge fund, Long-Term Capital Management (LTCM). As it appeared to be turning into a world crisis, attention was at long last drawn to the demerits of globalization. The outlook generally labeled the "Washington consensus" and mainstream economic thought as espoused by international financial institutions and the United States government, which until that time had expounded the principles of free trade as a universal panacea for development, now had to be revised. How has the crisis generally been understood, and how have East Asian countries coped with the implications of the crisis?

First, let us detail some facts about the crisis. It is now commonly understood that the currency and economic crisis started in Thailand in July 1997 as the result of a rapid outflow of short-term capital following a huge inflow in the first half of the 1990s. However, there is no common understanding of what caused the fast-paced outflow of short-term capital. Many neoclassical economists as well as the IMF, the United States government, and other official institutions usually stress internal factors as the main causes of the East Asian crisis. Nonmainstream economists and institutions such as the United Nations Conference on Trade and Development (UNCTAD), however, have serious doubts about interpretations stressing internal factors alone. They pay more attention to external factors. However, countries affected by the currency crisis had in general no other choice but to accept the conditions imposed by the IMF in order to receive emergency loans. The prescriptions the IMF imposed on the crisis-hit countries in East Asia included high interest rates for currency stability and a belt-tightening financial policy, both of which count as traditional prescriptions by the IMF, and other measures including a policy of liberalization of international trade regulations and structural reforms of domestic economies. The IMF in collaboration with the World Bank worked out these prescriptions.

The IMF imposed these policies because it interpreted the cause of the crisis as a weakness in the Asian capitalist model or East Asian structural problems of a systemic and organizational nature. Such an interpretation is typical of neoclassical economists who stress the role of the market, and was also that of the World Bank, the United States government, and financial institutions on Wall Street. According to the IMF, "a combination of inadequate financial sector supervision, poor assessment and management of financial risks, and the maintenance of relatively fixed exchange rates led banks and corporations to borrow large amounts of international capital, much of it short-term, denominated in foreign currency and unhedged. As time went on, this inflow of foreign capital tended to be used to finance poor quality investments" [IMF 1999a]. Inappropriate policies and/or systems made these countries fall into crisis. The interpretation of the Asian Development Bank (ADB) is the same: "These countries' economic success was built on a particular kind of economic strategy that emphasized export orientation, centralized coordination of production activities, and implicit (or even explicit) government guarantees of private investment projects, as well as a close operational relationship and interlinked ownership between banks and firms. Widely referred to as Asian industrial policy, this strategy allowed firms to rely heavily on bank credit. By international standards, firms in crisis-affected countries were extraordinarily highly leveraged" [ADB 1999: 26].

This interpretation became more persuasive by linking economic systems to authoritarian regimes and condemning them, calling countries exhibiting this kind of economic/political arrangement examples of crony capitalism, nepotism, and so on. At last, the prescriptions for combating crisis became consolidated into financial reforms and stricter guidelines on corporate governance.

The interpretation of the East Asian economic system and organization as the direct cause of the crisis gradually led to stress on policy errors. At the early stage of the crisis, interpretations stressing policy errors pointed at a prolonged exchange rate peg system during an excessive inflow of short-term capital, explicit and implicit guarantees by government for foreign and Asian domestic banks to lend and borrow large sums of money without regard to risk, an inadequate offshore currency market, and so forth. Liberalization itself was not seen as an error, but the sequencing of capital market liberalization was recognized as the main problem, which meant that weaknesses and vulnerabilities in domestic financial systems had to be addressed before further financial liberalization measures were to be pursued.

For example, Stanley Fischer, first deputy managing director of the IMF, answered a question at a press conference on March 10, 1998, saying that "the whole issue of whether or not liberalization was done properly, was sequenced properly, whether certain preconditions were met, I think is the issue that one needs to wrestle with. So I don't see it as negatively concluding about the general process of moving toward more open systems, but rather a question of how is the best way to do that" [IMF 1998]. The reason why the stress on the East Asian system or organization shifted to the sequencing of liberalization seems to be that the crisis could not be contained. It spread to Russia, countries in Latin America, and even to the New York Stock Exchange, which transformed it into a world crisis. If the former interpretation emphasizes the East Asian system or organization and the latter blames errors in the sequencing of liberalization, the keyword is still structural reform. The explanation changed but the remedy was the same.

By contrast, there is also an interpretation that points at hedge fund speculation, liquidity crisis, panic, or self-fulfilling financial crisis. This is 180 degrees different from the other two interpretations in terms of stressing external factors as the main cause. In 1997, the Malaysian Prime Minister Mohamad Mahathir was the only person with this view. He condemned a famous speculator, George Soros, because the hedge fund controlled by Soros had speculated against East Asian currencies. However, in 1998, Jagdish Bhagwati at Columbia University and the vice president of the World Bank, Joseph Stiglitz, MIT Professor Paul Krugman, and others also drew attention to the danger of capital account liberalization. They wrote that liberalization of trade in goods is not the same as liberalization of capital accounts, and the crises in East Asia and Latin America in the 1990s were self-fulfilling crises [Bhagwati et al. 1998]. Furthermore, once the famous U.S.-based hedge fund LTCM suffered near-collapse in September 1998 due to poor management of funds in Russia, much attention was paid to those activities of hedge funds thought to be lacking in transparency. Restriction on short-term capital movements began to be discussed among international economists and policy-makers.

The problem of restrictions on short-term capital was mainly discussed in the Committee on Banking Supervision at the Bank for International Settlements (BIS) in Basel. However, in the end, direct regulation on highly leveraged institutions (HLIs) themselves and/or exposure of their activities could not be realized because of opposition from the United States. Instead, the Basel Committee had to be satisfied that "many of the risks associated with the activities of HLIs can be addressed through better risk management processes at banks and securities firms." That is, it is considered sufficient that banking institutions assume the principal responsibility for managing their activities in a safe and prudent manner [BIS 1999, 2000]. In the final analysis, the reform of the international financial system is aimed at preventing systemic risk associated with free capital movement through the exposure of large banks. This is not the kind of regulation of the speculative activities of HLIs that many Asians had expected.

So, which interpretation of the crisis was adopted by East Asian countries and peoples? Of course, crisis-hit countries in East Asia did not have any choice, but had to accept the prescription imposed by the IMF. No matter how dissatisfied with the conditions imposed by the IMF, countries without enough political and economic power were forced to recognize "their own error." They might not be satisfied with the interpretation of the "Washington consensus" on the causes of the crisis while still going ahead with structural reforms. However, structural reforms themselves cannot prevent a crisis.

As interpretations of hedge fund speculation and/or self-fulfilling crises show, a regulation of short-term capital movement is needed when taking into account the reality of international financial markets with excess capital liquidity. This is a lesson drawn from the cases of Malaysian and Chinese capital control, and even the case of Singapore.[1] As long as international financial reforms do not include the regulation of free international financial transactions, governments have to pursue a unilateral solution to the problem of managing their currency and preventing financial crisis.

2.2 Capital Controls in Malaysia and Their Influence

The influence of Malaysia's experience with capital controls was strong on both developing and developed countries. However, at the beginning of the currency crisis, Malaysia carried out "a virtual IMF without the IMF loans," which included tight monetary and fiscal policies, raising the interest rate to defend the exchange rate, settling nonperforming loans, and other measures [Mahathir 2001: 26]. Such measures could not stop a depreciation in the Malaysian currency, the ringgit, so the Malaysian government adopted a fixed-rate system, pegging the ringgit at 3.8 to $1.00, and at the same time, imposing a "twelve month-rule" as a measure of capital control that prohibited the repatriation of portfolio funds for twelve months. Thanks to these measures, Malaysia's economy recovered rather smoothly. Because there was no outflow of short-term capital in September 1999, when the capital controls were removed, the IMF had to give credit to Malaysia's policy.[2]

At a summit meeting of the Asia-Pacific Economic Cooperation (APEC) forum held in Kuala Lumpur in November 1998, Malaysia, China, and Japan all tried to impose regulations on speculative transactions by hedge funds or similar institutions [*Nihon Keizai Shimbun* newspaper (NKS), November 11, 1998]. Although the control of speculative capital transactions could not be agreed upon by the APEC leaders as a result of strong opposition from the United States, the problem of regulations on free capital movement became a main point of discussion at international meetings such as IMF gatherings, an ASEM (Asia-Europe Meeting) finance ministers' meeting, G-7 summits and G-7 finance ministers' meetings. It was also dealt with intensively by the Basel Committee on Banking Supervision. In the end, the Basel Committee could not carry out direct regulations on free capital movements and supervision of such institutions as hedge funds. It only pursued public disclosure of banks and strengthened supervisory measures. However, at a meeting of G-7 finance ministers before the Cologne Summit, held in Frankfurt in June 1999, not only were controls on capital outflows agreed upon, but controls on capital inflows were also accepted, although only "in certain exceptional circumstances" [G-7 Finance Ministers 1999]. As long as the present international financial architecture did not impose any restrictions on free capital transactions under a policy of financial liberalization, summit leaders accepted some capital controls by governments, as in the case of Malaysia, in order to alleviate the dissatisfaction with capital liberalization in emerging economies.

In August, 1998, just when Malaysia was about to enforce controls on international capital movement, UNCTAD condemned the IMF's belt-tightening fiscal policy, writing that "tightening monetary policy may simply intensify the stampede, further undermining creditworthiness and increasing the risk of default." UNCTAD recommended that "debtor developing countries facing a speculative attack on their currencies should have the right to impose unilateral standstills on capital transactions like the trade safeguard actions permitted under WTO rules" [UNCTAD Press Release TAD/INF/2759]. Malaysia's capital controls, supported by UNCTAD, were ultimately successful in terms of economic recovery. As a result, some "breathing space" for developing countries in a globalizing financial world was gained.

As to exchange-rate systems, the view of the IMF changed, too. IMF senior research policy advisor Barry Eichengreen advocated the so-called "bipolar view," asserting that only two systems of flexible exchange system and currency union would be left in the twenty-first century, as he concluded in a study of the history of currency systems [Eichengreen 1994]. On the basis of this view, the IMF required developing countries to adopt a flexible exchange rate system when implementing a policy of liberalization. This became a precondition when the IMF extended a loan to developing countries. However, Malaysia chose a fixed exchange rate system to cope with the currency crisis, and a G-7 summit meeting accepted capital controls for crisis-hit countries. As a consequence, the IMF's new managing director, Horst Köhler, remarked that, "realistically, there is no alternative to floating exchange rates among the three major currencies. Looking beyond the three major currencies, an important conclusion of our research and reviews of country experience in the IMF is that no single exchange rate regime is appropriate for all members in all circumstances" [Köhler 2001].

The birth of the euro in Europe in January 1999 offered additional momentum for the East Asian countries to pay attention to currency stability and to recognize the necessity of a common currency. Japan again became interested in the internationalization of the yen. In April 1999, the Council on Foreign Exchange and Other Transactions of Japan's Ministry of Finance proposed to East Asian developing countries that a currency basket system, consisting of the dollar, yen, and euro, should be adopted in order to lessen exchange rate risks [Council 1999].

At a finance ministers' meeting of ASEAN+3 in May 1999, market stability and the use of the yen to strengthen economic relations between Japan and other East Asian countries were discussed. At the same time, a currency basket system proposed by Japan, was agreed. Although at present there are very few countries that have actually adopted a currency basket exchange rate system, it is important that such an agreement has been reached among the East Asian countries, and also that it has gained support from the IMF. Here we can easily see the influence of Malaysia's experience on the international economy.

However, crisis-hit countries and other countries in East Asia are still moving forward with liberalization and structural reforms following the prescriptions of the IMF and the World Bank while at the same time actively developing new policies. It is the first time in the history of East Asia that regional cooperation has been achieved. This will be discussed in the next section.

3. Development of Regional Financial Cooperation in East Asia

3.1 From Currency Crisis to Financial Cooperation

In August 1997, one month after the baht collapsed, a meeting to discuss emergency financial support to Thailand was organized by the IMF in Tokyo. Although the United States turned down an invitation to attend, the IMF and Japan agreed to make a support loan of $4 billion each, while the World Bank was to supply an additional $1.5 billion. In total the loans amounted to $17.2 billion. Supporters included Australia, Hong Kong, Singapore, Malaysia, Indonesia, Korea (Republic of Korea), and China.

There was a background of financial cooperation for the relief to Thailand. A tradition of Executives' Meeting of East Asia-Pacific Central Banks (EMEAP) was established in February 1991 among 11 central banks upon the initiative of the Bank of Japan. The initial purpose of the EMEAP was to exchange information on market developments in the economies of its members and it was to be a "forum for the Bank of Japan to brief others on Group of Seven discussions. But it has since evolved into quite a productive, and certainly the most active, forum for central banking discussions in the region to date through its biannual meetings of deputy governors and an annual meeting of governors" [Yam 1997: 9]. The first EMEAP Governors' Meeting, hosted by the Bank of Japan, was held in Tokyo in July 1996. At the second Governors' Meeting in Shanghai in July 1997, the group called for the creation of an "Asian Facility" to supplement IMF funding in providing assistance to member economies in Asia to facilitate structural adjustment.[3] "That historic decision paved the way for the smooth progression of the meeting organized by the IMF in Tokyo two weeks later in August when more than $10 billion, out of a total package of $17 billion to Thailand, was amassed from EMEAP members in a spirit of solidarity" [Yam 1997: 10]. In May 1997, the central banks of Thailand, Hong Kong, Singapore, and Malaysia jointly intervened in exchange markets to maintain the baht's value in response to speculative attack. When Indonesia faced a similar situation, Malaysia and Singapore also offered support. This was "a very meaningful gesture as well as solid support substantiating the vaguely "ASEAN spirit" [Sucharithanarugse 1998: 6].

In this context, the financial assistance to Thailand was a first step to substantial regional cooperation in East Asia. Development of regional cooperation could be said to be partly a reflection of economic integration in terms of trade and finance and partly a reflection of the necessity of strengthening regional cooperation.

Needless to say, financial support from the United States and official international institutions to crisis-hit countries was rather modest because they saw the weakness of the Asian system and organization, or policy errors, as the fundamental cause of the currency crisis. Therefore, the United States refused to attend the emergency meeting on financial support to Thailand in Tokyo. APEC, which advocated open regionalism, and even the ADB both took a more or less passive attitude. Looking at the "APEC Economic Outlook, 1997," out of 16 key achievements for 1997, only one was related to the financial crisis. It only said that "APEC agreed to examine ways to reduce the risks and better respond to the possibility of future financial crises in reaction to recent currency and stock market developments in the APEC region" [APEC 1997]. The "APEC Economic Outlook, 1998," written by the economic committee, had one section related to the crisis, titled "Commentaries on the Crisis: Highlights and Themes," in which it was said that "the analysis of the issues within APEC is broadly concordant with the views of other major international organizations." The economic committee included only simple summaries of the analyses of the crisis. At the 1997 APEC summit in Vancouver, an APEC Fund was proposed and was given a lukewarm response by the developed countries [Sucharithanarugse 1998: 7]. According to T.J. Pempel of the University of Washington, at the Vancouver meeting, "Participants did little to address the economic crisis, despite efforts by Philippine President Ramos to raise them. U.S. and Canadian representatives avoided the subject completely; Japan's delegation made it clear that it would not be 'so conceited' as to think it could be the region's locomotive. Only Chilean and Mexican leaders were interested in offering advice to their Asian counterparts—but, beyond advice, they could offer little more" [Pempel 1999: 229]. The 1999 annual report of the *Far Eastern Economic Review* [FEER 1999] noted that, "the Asian financial crisis sidelined the ADB and the APEC Forum, neither anticipated the depth of the crisis, and their role in coping with the situation was limited. They preferred to allow the IMF to make the running in bailing out the debt-ridden region. The ADB provided additional bailout funds for Indonesia, Korea and Thailand to assist in currency stabilization, while APEC's secretariat coordinated a few projects to develop regional capital markets" [FEER 1999: 36].

At an international conference on the "Future of Asia," organized by the NKS in June 2001, the former Deputy Prime Minister of Thailand, Supachai Panitchpakdi, asserted that, "Though in ASEAN, the ASEAN Free Trade Area (AFTA) has started and talks within APEC made progress, there was no so-called self-help cooperation program at the very serious period from 1997 to 2000. We promoted the ASEAN Investment Area, and introduced tariff reduction schemes. But, any systems could be used to solve the problems in the most important time. If we do not have a regional agreement to respond to the crisis, we cannot help mutually through a package for solving the problems" [Supachai 2001: 71].

This is an important critique of ASEAN's competence. ASEAN has already had the "ASEAN Swap Arrangement" set up by the ASEAN central banks and monetary authorities in August 1977 to assist member countries "to bridge temporary international liquidity problems in times of crisis" [ASEAN Secretariat 1995: 15]. However, the swap arrangement, which provided credit at about $45–65 million to ASEAN member countries between 1985 and 1987 [UNCTAD 1996: 111], was too small in volume to cope with the 1997 crisis [Hirakawa 2002]. That is, APEC, which ought to be a forum for regional cooperation, did not have a serious interest in assisting crisis-hit countries; the cooperation framework of ASEAN was also too small and lacking in power. Such realities forced East Asian countries to realize the necessity of a new framework of regional cooperation. For this reason, "Interest in regional financial arrangements and cooperation in the developing world has increased rapidly since the outbreak of the Asian crisis" [UNCTAD 2001: 121].

3.2 From an Asian Monetary Fund to the New Miyazawa Initiative

A new move toward monetary cooperation in East Asia originated in Japan. In response to requests from Thailand during the crisis, Japan first proposed an Asian Monetary Fund (AMF) at the Tokyo meeting for emergency financial support in August 1997.[4] Initially, it was designed as a regional institution giving emergency financial support to crisis-hit countries, which would be independent from the IMF [NKS, November 24, 1997]. The following month, the idea was proposed at an

ASEM finance ministers' meeting held in Bangkok, an informal meeting of Japan-ASEAN finance ministers in Hong Kong, and during a series of international meetings on financial issues, including the IMF–World Bank Annual Meeting and a G-7 Meeting. The funding was later increased to $100 billion, half of which was to come from Japan and the remainder from China, Hong Kong, Singapore, and Taiwan [ADB 1999: 44; Hirakawa 2001: 18–21].

However, this idea came to an end at the Manila meeting of proxies of finance ministers and central bank governors from 14 countries, held November 18–19, 1997, as a result of the stiff opposition from the United States and the IMF, even though Malaysia supported it strongly. Instead, the "Manila framework" was chosen, serving to strengthen the IMF's capacity to respond to financial crises and also establishing a mechanism for regional surveillance.

As to the reasons why the United States and the IMF opposed an AMF, the *Wall Street Journal* explained that "Mr. Rubin, Treasury Secretary, and Mr. Summers, Deputy Treasury Secretary, feared the fund would offer big loans with less-stringent conditions than the IMF's and would threaten U.S. economic supremacy. Treasury officials worked the corridors of Hong Kong's convention center and the city's private dining rooms to slow the Japanese plan's momentum. China, Korea, and other nations suspicious of Tokyo's ambitions leaned toward the U.S.... A victorious Mr. Summers declared afterward, "U.S. economic leadership is crucial to avoid a descent into the kind of regionalism and protectionism that we saw in the periods between the first and second world wars"" [*Wall Street Journal*, September 24,1998].

Despite this setback, about one year later, on October 3, 1998, Japan, again announced a "New Initiative to Overcome the Asian Currency Crisis," totaling $30 billion. It carried the name of "The New Miyazawa Initiative," after Finance Minister Kiichi Miyazawa. On October 6, at the 53rd IMF–World Bank Joint Annual Discussion, Miyazawa criticized the IMF approach in a statement read by the Japanese State Secretary of Finance: "Asking a country with a fiscal surplus to tighten further, or asking a country to take a high interest rate policy for the sake of exchange rate protection, could end up with more negatives than positives... inviting a downturn in the economy, and further eroding confidence" [Miyazawa 1998].

The New Miyazawa Initiative was accepted with much goodwill by crisis-hit countries. Thailand's Finance Minister Tarrin Nimmanahaeminda said that the plan was more substantial than the Japan-sponsored Asian Monetary Fund of a year before because the specific provisions offered by Japan amounted to more than just a substantial sum of money. Bank of Indonesia Governor Sjahril Sabrin said, "This really shows the effort by the Japanese to lead recovery of the Asian countries" [Dow Jones News Service, October 3, 1998]. Moreover, both the vice director of the World Bank, Joseph Stiglitz, and Jeffrey Sachs of Harvard University supported the initiative. Fred Bergsten, director of the Institute for International Economics, even accepted the necessity of an AMF [Bergsten 1998].

In May 1999, the second stage of the New Miyazawa Initiative, labeled "Resource Mobilization Plan for Asia," was announced. The Japanese government declared credit guarantees for public bonds issued by Asian countries as well as the intention to acquire such bonds. Although the second stage of the New Miyazawa

Initiative was received unfavorably by East Asian countries, under the Initiative, as of February 2, 2000, total support amounted to $21 billion. Japan also contributed $362.5 million to the ADB under the same scheme, and in March 1999 the ADB approved the establishment of the Asian Currency Crisis Support Facility (ACCSF) to help Asia's currency-crisis-hit countries [ADB News Release 14/99].

The New Miyazawa Initiative was aimed at helping governments and firms affected by the crisis to restructure corporate debt, stabilize financial systems, strengthen the social safety net, and address the credit crunch. The facilities can be seen as a supplier of funds to East Asian countries in a process of economic recovery. However, it differs from the AMF even if it is an alternative to it. The AMF was conceived as a regional international institution. By contrast, the Miyazawa Initiative is a bilateral scheme of cooperation. In addition, not only currency stability in East Asia but also the internationalization of the yen came in sight more clearly with the Miyazawa Initiative than with the AMF. Therefore, the idea of an AMF was soon revived among countries in East Asia.

3.3 From the Internationalization of the Yen to Regional Currency and Financial Cooperation

The year 1999 saw the advent of the euro, which impressed upon Japan the economic difficulty of currency stability. On the first day of the euro, Finance Minister Miyazawa stated, "Today marks the birth of a new currency, the euro, which I very much welcome. This is a great step towards a closer economic and monetary union." At the same time, he referred to the internationalization of the yen: "We acknowledge the importance of the internationalization of the yen in light of global economic and financial developments such as the Asian financial crisis" [Miyazawa 1999].

The Japanese government had taken steps toward the internationalization of the yen as early as the 1980s. The Japan Offshore Market (JOM) was established in 1986 and the Tokyo International Financial Futures Market (TIFFM) in 1989. However, by 1999, a sense of crisis in response to the currency crisis in East Asia and the birth of the euro in Europe motivated the Japanese government to further action. The Council on Foreign Exchange and Other Transactions at the Ministry of Finance submitted a report entitled "Internationalization of the Yen for the 21st Century," and took the view that "The strengthening of the international role of the yen will contribute to the stability of foreign exchange markets, particularly those in Asia, and to the stability of Asian Economies."[5] The Council proposed a "system which stabilizes Asian currency exchange rates against a currency basket containing the dollar, yen, euro, and other currencies" [Council 1999].

For other countries in East Asia that rely on an export-oriented development policy, the stability of currency is of decisive importance. Furthermore, these countries often have a so-called triangle structure in trade, balancing huge deficits with Japan and surpluses with the United States. This means that they are faced with the difficulty of procuring yen. However, their share in trade with Japan has not been so great. The share accounted for by Japan in total exports of East Asian countries in 1999 was only 11%, against a share of 23% for the United States and 15% for Europe [JETRO Trade Matrix]. Considering that Japan's share of world GDP is about 14%, the Japan's share in exports from other East Asian countries is rather small. In addition, Japan has regulated trading in the yen on the international offshore market for a long time. It seemed more rational to use the dollar. Nevertheless, dollar-pegged exchange rate systems in East Asian countries brought them to crisis. Therefore, the predicaments of currency crisis and the birth of the euro brought other East Asian countries, as well as Japan, to acknowledge the need for greater stability for their currencies.

Prime Minister Mahathir Mohamad of Malaysia claimed on January 11, 1999, that an international currency was now also needed in Asia. He said that the yen should shoulder that role [*Mainichi Shimbun* newspaper, January 12, 1999]. On the same day, according to the *Japan Times,* some central bankers also expressed the opinion that "A single currency for Asia might someday be in the cards," although they were "far from ready to seriously consider such a step" [Hirakawa 1999: 390]. At a JETRO conference in February 1999, the former Deputy Prime Minister of Thailand, Virabongsa Ramangkura, also referred to an Asian Fund and the internationalization of the yen [Ramangkura 1999: 10]. At a meeting of finance ministers of ASEAN+3, held in Manila in May 1999, there was agreement on using the yen for market stability and for strengthening economic relations between Japan and other East Asian countries. They also expressed approval for a currency basket systems using the dollar, yen, euro, and other currencies [NKS, May 1, 1999].

It is, however, very difficult for East Asian countries to accept the internationalization of the yen. China, for example, opposes this idea strongly, because of feelings against Japan that stem from the historical experience of Japanese occupation.[6] Nevertheless, a regional framework for currency stability for East Asian countries is indispensable. Since the currency crisis occurred in countries where short-term debt had exceeded international reserves, sound macroeconomic policy and confidence in the market are important as well. Yet, "no matter how much liquidity a country holds, this amount is dwarfed by the magnitude of international capital flows and a country alone cannot protect itself against the attack of international capital" [Moon et al. 2000: 163]. Once a crisis takes place somewhere, huge amounts of capital will flow out of the area. Developing countries can hardly expect the IMF to provide relief for such liquidity crises.[7] There is, therefore, no other option but to aim for international liquidity through regional cooperation. The ASEAN countries and Korea have also urged regional financial cooperation in East Asia.

The idea of an AMF, although rejected, was revived in 1999. In the press it was said, that "Japan's concept of an Asian Monetary Fund, though withdrawn by Tokyo after IMF criticism, was resuscitated in a forum of Asian finance ministers. Known as the "Manila framework," the forum called for a cooperative financing arrangement to supplement IMF funding" [FEER 1999: 38]. At the ASEAN+3 informal summit held in Manila in November 1999, the region's leaders agreed to strengthen and enhance "self-help and support mechanisms in monetary and financial cooperation, in East Asia through the ASEAN+3 Framework" [ASEAN+3 Summit 1999].

In response to this agreement, the ASEAN+3 finance ministers' meeting held in Chiang Mai, Thailand, in May 2000, adopted the expanded ASEAN swap arrangement including China, Japan, and Korea. This "Chiang Mai Initiative" would strengthen existing cooperative frameworks among monetary authorities. However, the initiative is considered to be a step toward an "AMF" in the future[8] and even to a future common currency.

At the ADBI/FIMA Symposium "From the Asian Financial Crisis of 1997 to a Regional Financing Arrangement" held in Hawaii in May 2001, the following prediction was made: "The most important changes to the world's financial architecture are likely to come from the new regional arrangements being realized in East Asia by Japan, China, Korea, and the ten member countries of ASEAN. The idea of a multilateral cooperation agreement has been revived again on May 6, 2000, when the finance ministers of the ASEAN+3 countries met in Chiang Mai." Moreover, the prediction gives a definite and hopeful timeframe for the new international financial architecture to materialize. "Within a decade pursuant to the time when the multicurrency placements will have been made, regional financial cooperation and institutionalization will have grown to a point where a common currency area will become a viable and realistic option for East Asia" [Chaipravat 2001: 4–5, 9]. At the International Conference "Monetary Outlook on East Asia in an Integrating World Economy," held in September 2001 in Bangkok, one monetary expert from the ADB made a presentation about a common currency for ASEAN and concluded that "The increased pace of globalization is likely to encourage the formation of currency unions.... Overall, events may become more favorable to the formation of currency unions" [Madhur 2001: 8].

One researcher at the Thailand Development Research Institute Foundation discussed the necessity of a "regional lender of last resort," preferring this term to the aforementioned "AMF." He used the analogy of the relationship between regional development banks and the World Bank. He said that a regional lender of last resort is needed even if the IMF exists, just as regional banks are needed even though there is a World Bank [Vichyanond 2000]. Masaru Yoshitomi at the ADB institute not only acknowledged the necessity of a regional lender but also offered a long-term overview of the future of currencies in East Asia: "After 50 years, the currency system in East Asia could change to multiple currency basket and common basket systems, and come to a single currency" [Yoshitomi 2001: 131–133].

The experience of the European Community teaches that currency fluctuations associated with floating exchange rate systems increase transaction costs when regional integration progresses further. This implies a greater necessity for building a stable exchange rate system and establishing a common response to the dollar. If a regional common currency is installed, "they [the East Asian countries] can reduce the transaction costs of doing business within a region and eliminate exchange rate spreads and commissions in currency trading associated with international trade and investment" [UNCTAD 2001: 124]. The prospect of moving from regional financial cooperation to common currency is now emerging.

4. Globalization and the Development of Regionalism in East Asia

4.1 Development of Regional Economic Cooperation in East Asia

Currency and financial cooperation has progressed in the wake of the Asian crisis, contrary to general expectations that regional collaboration would be very difficult to realize as a result of the diverse interests of East Asian countries and strong mutual distrust, especially in Northeast Asia. Needless to say, this is only one part of regional cooperation. Since the crisis, East Asia has gone beyond financial cooperation to economic cooperation; the pace of regionalism has accelerated.[9]

With a 1985 white paper entitled "Completing the Internal Market: White Paper from the Commission to the European Council" providing momentum, interest in regionalism has grown all over the world. With the Treaty of Maastricht, signed in 1992, the European Union attained complete market integration in 1993 and the common currency, the euro, was introduced in 1999. From January 1, 2002, domestic currencies were replaced by euros in a "Euroland" consisting of 12 countries.[10] On the American continent, the United States signed the U.S.–Canada Free Trade Agreement in 1989 and the North America Free Trade Agreement (NAFTA) was concluded by the United States, Canada, and Mexico in 1992 and became effective in 1993. As of 2001, the European Union, with a GDP of $7,884 billion, embraces 15 countries with a total population of 377.4 million, while NAFTA has a GDP of $11,466 billion, consists of three countries, and has a combined population of 414.4 million.

Moreover, these regional agreements are being enlarged. The EU has recently agreed to incorporate a number of Eastern European countries into the union. The EU signed the EU–South Africa Trade, Development and Co-operation Agreement (TDCA) in January 2001, and the Mexico–EU Free Trade Agreement with Mexico in July 2001. Similarly, in the western hemisphere, at the summit of the Americas held in Miami in December 1994, the initiative was taken to establish a single free trade agreement. Leaders attending the summit agreed to complete negotiations toward building a Free Trade Agreement of the Americas (FTAA) by 2005. At the second summit of the Americas, in Santiago, Chile, formal FTAA negotiations were launched, and at the sixth meeting of Ministers of Trade of the western hemisphere, in April 2001, agreement was reached to bring the FTAA into force according to the original plan [FTAA website http://www.ftaa].

By contrast, until the middle of the 1990s, only the ASEAN countries had made any movement toward regionalism in East Asia. The first person to take action was Malaysia's Prime Minister Mahathir, who proposed an East Asia Economic Group (EAEG) in December 1990. After the EAEG had changed its name to the East Asia Economic Caucus (EAEC), in response to opposition from the United States, its importance was reaffirmed at the Fourth ASEAN Summit in January 1992. Nevertheless, since the EAEC members were the ASEAN countries, Japan, China and Korea, i.e., the same as in the EAEG, the initiative was afterwards criticized.[11] Therefore, not much progress was made until ASEAN+3 meetings came into being late in the 1990s. ASEAN+3 meetings began in the midst of the crisis, and the first joint statement on East Asian cooperation in history was issued in November 1999, so naturally the relationship between the EAEC and ASEAN+3 attracted attention.

Incidentally, there had been two important previous steps apart from the proposal for EAEG or EAEC before the ASEAN+3 summit meetings started. The initial step was the first ASEM, held in Bangkok in March 1996, when leaders of Japan, China, and Korea and ASEAN countries' representatives attended the meeting as Asian participants. The second step was the proposal by Japanese Prime Minister Ryutaro Hashimoto to ASEAN during a trip to Southeast Asia in January 1997 to hold regular Japan–ASEAN summit meetings.[12] At that time, Japan tried to strengthen its defense powers during the review of the Japan–United States Guidelines for Defense Cooperation. China kept a strict watch on Japan's defense policy. In terms of Japan's diplomacy, one of the aims was to promote relations with ASEAN in order to form a counterweight to China [NKS, January 20 1997]. In part it aimed to explain Japan's defense policy and to alleviate the apprehension of ASEAN countries toward Japan [*Asahi Shimbun* newspaper, January 6, 1997]. However, ASEAN leaders showed a preference for strengthening balanced relations with both Japan and China rather than only with Japan. Consequently, ASEAN made a counterproposal for an ASEAN+3 summit meeting, which was realized by ASEAN inviting the leaders of Japan, China, and the Korea to the 30th anniversary ASEAN summit in December 1997.

The first ASEAN+3 summit meeting thus was held in the middle of the currency crisis. As a matter of course, participants at the meeting agreed to cooperate toward currency and financial stability. At the Sixth ASEAN Summit in Hanoi in December 1998, the leaders of ASEAN and the three countries decided "on the importance of holding a regular meeting among them and recognizing the ongoing efforts of the East Asia Vision Group." At the ASEAN+3 summit meeting in Manila in November 1999, the framework of ASEAN+3 developed further.

It was agreed "to enhance this dialogue process and strengthen cooperation with a view to advancing East Asian collaboration" [ASEAN+3 Summit 1999]. At this meeting, "the ASEAN+3 leaders underscored their commitment to build upon existing consultative and cooperative processes, as well as joint efforts." Fields of economic cooperation included information technology, e-commerce, strengthening small- and medium-sized enterprises (SMEs), industry, and agricultural cooperation as well as cooperation in trade and investment. In the area of monetary and financial cooperation, participants called for reforms to international financial architecture and the enhancement of self-help and support mechanisms in East Asia through the ASEAN+3 framework [ASEAN+3 Summit 1999]. In this context, the East Asian Vision Group, initiated by Korean President Dae Jung Kim, was created in October 1999. A vision report, "Towards an East Asian Community," was submitted to leaders of ASEAN+3 countries in October 2001, in which the formation of an "East Asian community" was proposed [EAVG 2001].

At the ASEAN+3 Finance Ministers' meeting held in Chiang Mai in May 2000, the ASEAN+3 Swap Arrangement, i.e. the Chiang Mai Initiative mentioned above, was concluded. At the Fourth ASEAN+3 Summit meeting in Singapore in November 2000, the chairman, Singapore's Prime Minister Chok Tong Goh, proposed an East Asian summit instead of an ASEAN+3 Summit, which had taken the form of ASEAN inviting the other three leaders. An East Asian Free Trade and Investment Zone was also discussed [*Asahi Shimbun* newspaper; NKS, November 25, 2000].

In November 2001, the Fifth ASEAN+3 Summit was held in Bandar Seri Begawan, Brunei, but now the interest in economic cooperation appeared to have weakened, especially in Japan, as a result of the terrorist attacks of September 11 in the United States. However, the Report of the Vision Group was cited by Korean President Kim who "highlighted proposals to set up an East Asian forum and the responsibility of an East Asian summit. The study group is now assessing the proposal." The proposal was scheduled to be submitted in Cambodia in 2002. China, Japan and Korea also agreed to support ASEAN in the effort to accelerate ASEAN integration [ASEAN+3 Summit 2001].

In the wake of the currency crisis, East Asia at long last has started to act as a cohesive region with the formation of ASEAN+3 meetings, a framework that was earlier opposed by the United States, thereby responding to the challenge of regionalism spreading throughout Europe and the western hemisphere. Of course, it has not yet become an East Asian summit in the true sense of the word with an organization of its own but it has at least met regularly. East Asia's regional cooperation has thus gained acceptance both inside and outside East Asia.

4.2 Free Trade Agreements and the ASEAN/Korea Initiative

Mainstream economics has discussed free trade agreements (FTAs) or regional trade agreements (RTAs) in relation to the General Agreement on Tariffs and Trade (GATT)—the World Trade Organization (WTO)'s multilateral trading system. This is called regionalism and has been met with much skepticism.[13] Nevertheless, FTAs increased rapidly in number in the 1990s. Table 1, based on information from the Japan External Trade Organization (JETRO), shows an FTA boom in the second half of the 1990s. Ninety percent of FTA agreements now in effect were signed in the 1990s and 95% within one region alone, namely Europe. Even if we exclude FTAs formed in Russia, Middle and Eastern Europe, the Commonwealth of Independent States (CIS), and Africa, the remaining European countries, including the Near and Middle East, still account for 74 of the FTAs formed in 1950–2003. Moreover, there is also the huge NAFTA bloc in the western hemisphere, i.e., there is a heavy concentration in Europe and the Americas.

A variety of reasons for joining an FTA are pointed out by the WTO. Economic benefits include the creation of economies of scale, competition forcing domestic manufacturers to produce goods more efficiently, and faster and deeper liberalization. Political benefits include preventing countries from going to war with one another, consolidating domestic economic reforms and providing political stability, and increasing the bargaining power of smaller countries. And as a combination of economic and political benefits, there is the acceleration of liberalization [http://wto.org].

Table 1. Number of free trade agreements registered with the GATT/WTO (through May 5, 2003).

	Intraregional FTAs			Cross-regional FTAs				
Date of Notification	Within Europe	Within the Americas	Within Asia	Europe-Americas	Europe-Asia	Asia-Americas	Europe-Americas-Asia	Total
1950–1959	1	0	0	0	0	0	0	1
1960–1969	1	1	0	1	1	0	0	4
1970–1979	9	1	2	0	0	0	1	13
1980–1989	1	2	2	1	0	0	1	7
1990–1994	25	2	3	0	0	0	0	30
1995–1999	55	2	1	0	0	0	0	58
2000–2003	27	2	3	1	2	0	0	35
Total	119	10	11	3	3	0	2	148
	140 (95 %)			8 (5 %)				(100 %)

The number of FTAs registered with the World Trade Organization (WTO) is the total number notified based on Article XXIV of the General Agreement on Tariffs and Trade (GATT) and the enabling clause. "Europe" includes Russia, the Near and Middle East, and Africa; "Asia" includes Oceania; "Americas" includes North and South America, and the Caribbean Islands

Source: JETRO's WTO/FTA Column (No. 15, July 30, 2003) which is based on WTO's FTA List (as of May 5, 2003)

East Asia was the last region where the movement of regionalism spread. According to the Japan External Trade Organization (JETRO), Japan, China, Korea, Taiwan, and Hong Kong were not members of any FTA in 2001 [JETRO 2001a]. At the Fourth ASEAN Summit in 1992, it was decided to establish the ASEAN Free Trade Area (AFTA) by 2008 in order to promote greater direct investment and intra-ASEAN trade. In 1994 ASEAN agreed to reduce the initial time frame from 15 to 10 years to accelerate the establishment of the FTA.[14] FTAs in East Asia are as yet limited to ASEAN, however.

Moreover, in East Asia, the APEC informal ministerial meeting held in Indonesia in November 1994 resulted in the Bogor Declaration to aim for free trade and open investment by 2010 for developed economies and by 2020 for developing economies. In January 1995, the WTO, successor to GATT, came into being, which seemed to strengthen the world trading system.

Nevertheless, after the crisis, Singapore, Thailand, and Korea pushed forward with FTAs, i.e., regionalism in the sense of the WTO definition[15] (Fig. 1). The first step was Korean President Kim's proposal to then-Japanese Prime Minister Keizo Obuchi of a Korea–Japan free trade agreement in October 1998.[16] According to a communiqué from the two leaders in November 1998, institutes in each country, the JETRO–Institute of Developing Economies (IDE) in Japan and the Korea Institute for International Economic Policies (KIEP) in Korea, would set up study teams for a joint examination of future economic relations, including the possibility of establishing a free trade agreement. In May 2000, the two institutes brought out a joint communiqué entitled "Towards Closer Japan–Korea Economic Relations: Proposal Formulating a 21st Century Partnership." In December 2001, one Korean minister

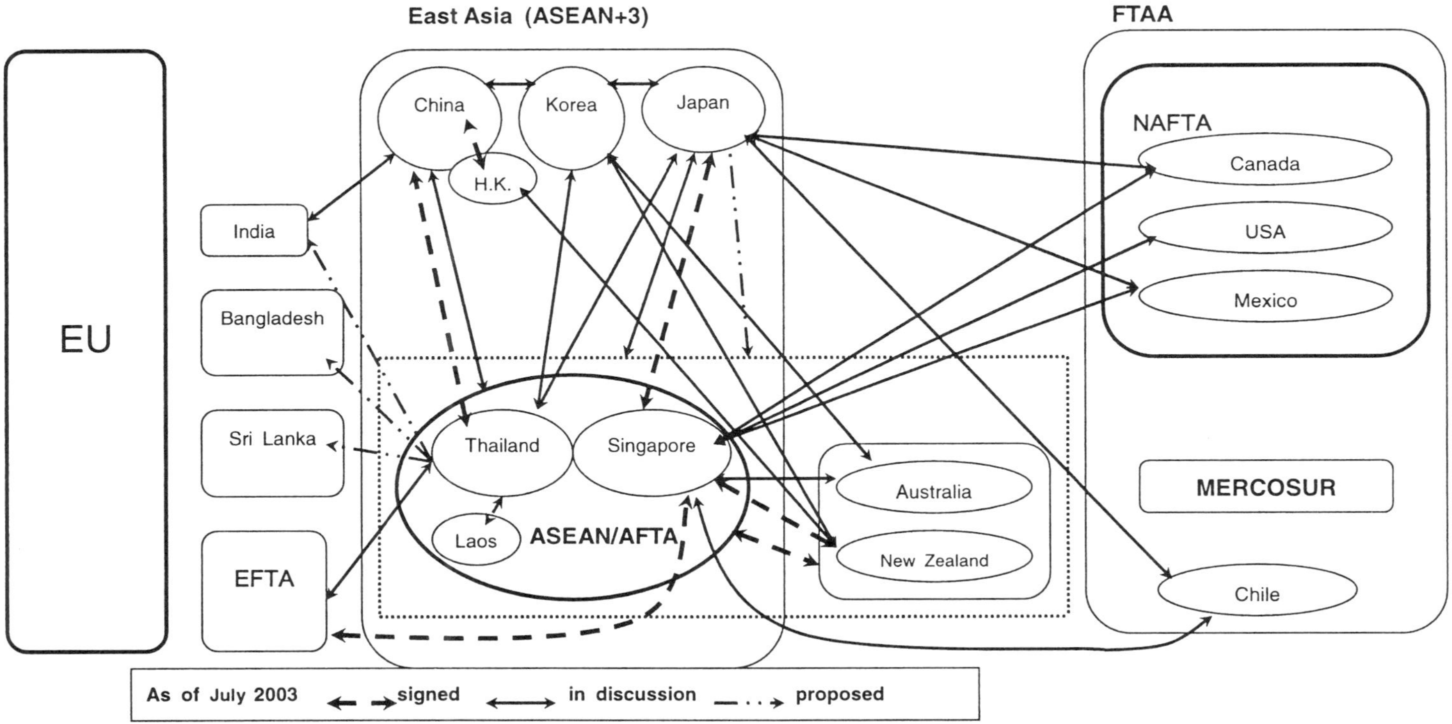

Fig. 1. Correlations of free trade agreements for East Asian countries. Note: Thailand may seek FTAs with Australia, New Zealand, China, Mexico, the Czech Republic, Croatia, and Egypt. In addition to the countries shown in the figure, Japan has created a task force to study the FTA with the Philippines and Malaysia. Japan is also planning to start preliminary negotiations with Indonesia. China has proposed a Japan–China–Korea FTA

announced that a Japan–Korea investment agreement could be expected in the very near future [NKS, December 15, 2001]. Further, Korea is now discussing FTAs with Australia, New Zealand, and Mexico, as well as with Japan and China.

In the ASEAN region, Singapore is very active. Following Korea, in December 1999, it proposed an FTA with Japan, and a joint study on an FTA was agreed by the leaders of the two countries. In September 2000, a joint report was submitted. On January 13, 2002, the Japan–Singapore FTA was signed in Singapore.[17] Singapore had already agreed on an FTA with New Zealand in November 2000. It has been discussing an FTA with Chile since November 1999, with Canada since June 2000, with Mexico since July 2000, with the United States since November 2000, and with Australia since February 2001. Exploratory talks have been initiated between Singapore and the EFTA (Lichtenstein, Norway, and Switzerland) [http://secretariat.efta.int/news/2001].

The second active country with respect to FTAs is Thailand. According to Kyodo News, "Thailand may seek FTAs with Korea, Australia, New Zealand, China, Mexico, India, the Czech Republic, Croatia and Egypt in 2001 [Kyodo News, February 28, 2001; April 5, 2001]. To Japan, Thai Prime Minister Thaksin proposed a study on the possibility of establishing an FTA during his visit to Japan in November 2001 [NKS, November 20, 2001]. In addition, he had meetings in New Delhi in January 2002 and intends to conclude FTAs within 10 years with India, Myanmar, Bangladesh, and Sri Lanka [NKS, December 31, 2001].

There is a tentative list of "FTAs in the process of discussion as of September 2001," compiled by the Japanese Ministry of Economy, Trade and Industry (METI). According to this list, 19 cases are in the process of discussion, of which eight cases (42%) are related to East Asia including six related to Singapore, one to Korea, and one to Hong Kong. Starting points were late 1999 for the earlier cases, and from 2000 to early 2001 for the rest.

Furthermore, according to the list of those at the proposal stage, there are 15 cases, of which eight (53%) relate to East Asia including three involving Singapore, three Korea, and one each for Thailand and China. Singapore and Thailand are clearly very active in this process. Korea also shows a tendency toward becoming more active.

Why are FTAs on the increase in East Asia? One possible reason is the increasing number of people skeptical about rapid globalization; another is the delay and disappointment with the liberalization process by the WTO, signified by the failure of the Third WTO Ministerial Conferece in Seattle. In addition, FTAs are seen as a means of providing market access, especially in the case of an FTA with large markets, "as a way of avoiding the imposition of possible protectionist measures in the future [with regard to the United States], and managing future trade tensions" [Rajan et al. 2001: 9]. Scollay and Gilbert explain the proliferation of FTAs as follows. The Early Voluntary Sectoral Liberalization (EVSL) initiative,[18] which the APEC leaders recognized in Vancouver in 1997, had a disappointing outcome at the end of 1998. Therefore, a reassessment of the prospect for successful liberalization within the APEC process was made. The rise of FTAs should not be linked to disillusionment with the WTO process [Scollay and Gilbert 2001: 7].

In the wake of the currency crisis, countries in East Asia, especially Singapore, seem to think that liberalization through the multilateral trading system of the WTO alone cannot form a counterweight against the markets in the United States (and elsewhere in NAFTA) and Europe, where regional FTAs have made great strides. This may be a reason why trans-regional FTAs are being pursued. By contrast, FTAs within East Asia seem to have two main reasons for existing. One is political: an increase in bargaining power vis-à-vis the United States and the European Union. The second reason is the need for enlargement of regional markets. Through FTAs, regional cooperation will move forward.

Of course, as will be discussed below, not every country in East Asia agreed with the need for FTAs. Nonetheless, as long as they realize that they can not adopt protectionist policies, regional cooperation through FTAs, which precedes regional integration, is seen as a better way to develop. This is one important lesson from the currency crisis.

The main promoters of FTAs are Singapore, Thailand, and increasingly Korea. In terms of regional cooperation, ASEAN and Korea attract the most attention. ASEAN+3 meetings came into being through an ASEAN invitation to the other three countries. Here the initiative by the Malaysian Prime Minister Mahathir cannot be overlooked. In promoting regional cooperation after the crisis, ASEAN, in particular Singapore, Malaysia, and Thailand, and also Korea have made important moves. We may call this an ASEAN/Korea Initiative. In response to this, Japan, as a major economic power, and China, as a major political power, have begun to move toward regional cooperation too.

4.3 East Asia's Free Trade Agreements and Japan and China

Until recently, Japan gave priority to the multilateral trading system of GATT/WTO, and did not participate in any regional or bilateral FTA. The reason was the Japanese view that trade protectionism was one factor that led to the world wars in the first half of the twentieth century. Because the GATT system has been advantageous to Japan with its strong export orientation, Japan was apprehensive about trade protectionism. In addition to this, Japan has difficulty with regional cooperation policies because some East Asian countries, especially China and Korea, are strongly critical of Japan because of its occupation of parts of East Asia before and during the Second World War. However, Japan has since changed its view of FTAs and has shown a markedly increased interest in regional trade agreements after the Asian crisis.

This policy change was first officially expressed in the "White Paper on International Trade" issued in 2000. This document discussed the reasons for an FTA policy in terms of a detailed theoretical and empirical analysis of regional integration. Theoretical analysis traditionally had a tendency to focus on the "static effects" of trade creation and trade diversion. However, it is important to consider also the "dynamic effects," i.e., the impact on economic growth brought about through a higher level of productivity and capital accumulation, and effects in "promoting direct investment and encouraging policy reform." The latter are labeled direct investment promotion effects and policy reform effects, and are based on empirical analysis of existing regional blocs. In conclusion, METI's White Paper 2000 stated that FTAs could complement the WTO system [METI 2000]. Japan thus undertook to pursue "multi-layered external economic policies" [METI 2001: 221]. JETRO also expressed the same views, stressing the positive effects of FTAs on both the Japanese and the world economy. "Free trade agreements (FTAs) complement the WTO-centered multilateral free trade system. In addition to having a positive impact on trade and investment, FTAs stimulate domestic regulatory reform and prevent backtracking" [JETRO 2001c: 28].

Several countries, for instance Korea and Singapore, have also called for a change in Japanese policy toward FTAs. Korea's first proposal to Japan in October 1998 was followed by proposals for FTAs and/or investment agreements with Mexico in November 1998, Chile in October 1999, Singapore in December 1999, and Australia in October 2000. Despite opposition to the negotiations that meant that no start could be made until the autumn of 2000, the ASEAN Secretary-General also urged Japan to study the possibility of an ASEAN–Japan FTA [NKS, January 14, 2002].

China also moved to link up with the FTA boom. At the ASEAN+3 summit meeting in Singapore in November 2000, Chinese Premier Rhongji Zhu raised the prospect of a China–ASEAN free trade zone to strengthen trade and investment links with ASEAN [Latelinenews.com, November 25, 2000]. According to the *People's Daily,* Zhu said that China attaches great importance to developing relations of cooperation, partnership, good neighborliness, and mutual trust with ASEAN [*People's Daily* online, November 24, 2000].

However, in response to China's proposal, Singapore's Prime Minister Goh proposed another idea for an FTA, the Greater East Asian Economic Zone, and called for a study of the possibility of such a zone by ASEAN members and the Chinese, Korean, and Japanese leaders [*Korea Herald*, November 27, 2000; NKS November 25, 2000]. ASEAN feared intensified competition with China when it established the ASEAN Free Trade Area and tried to counter pressure from China's by strengthening ties with Japan.[19] Geopolitics brought forward the idea of regional integration in East Asia, which was discussed and studied at the ASEAN+3 meetings.

Nevertheless, Japan's passivity and China's positive attitude to a greater East Asian free trade zone led to contrasting results for the two countries at the ASEAN meeting in Brunei in November 2001. At the ASEAN–China summit meeting, China agreed to start talks on the formation of an ASEAN–China FTA within 10 years. By contrast, Japan, with a greater interest in world politics and also trying to appease the United States, failed to issue an antiterrorism joint statement there.[20]

One of Japan's leading newspapers, the *Asahi Shimbun* newspaper, commented on China's vigorous policy toward an FTA with ASEAN in an article entitled "ASEAN, China bypass Japan," which originated from a Thai source just before the ASEAN+3 Summit in Brunei. The *Asahi Shimbun* newspaper expressed worries about Japan's isolation in East Asia.[21] The NKS also reported on this under the title "China is trying to enclose ASEAN." It said that, since China proposed an FTA with

ASEAN, China is aiming to strengthen relations with ASEAN [NKS, November 2, 2001]. Furthermore, "in order to talk to ASEAN, which entertains a fear of China's economic power, and agree to an FTA within 10 years, China adopted a two-step policy. First, China would liberalize her domestic market of agricultural goods to ASEAN products. After a while, ASEAN would decide the liberalization of its manufactured goods market. It is the principle that the nation with power should make sacrifices first" [*Asahi Shimbun* newspaper, November 7, 2001].

Needless to say, China's attitude forced a change in Japan's policy toward East Asia, encouraging Japan to push forward with a new proposal. Japanese Prime Minister Junichiro Koizumi visited various ASEAN countries to propose the Japan–ASEAN Comprehensive Economic Partnership in January 2002. Koizumi emphasized the importance of security, as reflected in the terrorist attacks of September 11. The areas to be covered by the partnership were extended from trade and investment to science and technology, human resources development, and tourism. However, in this proposal, Australia and New Zealand were added to the member countries of ASEAN+3 as core member countries. Along with this, Koizumi said that his proposed community should forge a partnership with other regions of the world, particularly the United States, and that it would be better not to have a time limit on FTA talks and to tackle the liberalization of trade in agricultural products on a case-by-case basis [NKS, January 14, 2002]. Koizumi's attitude toward the Japan–ASEAN Comprehensive Economic Partnership has many problems for the promotion of an East Asian FTA.

Moreover, in the 6th ASEAN+3 Summit Meeting in Phnom Penh in November 2002, Cambodia, ASEAN–China FTA negotiation progressed further. The ASEAN and Chinese leaders signed the Framework Agreement on ASEAN–China Economic Cooperation, which will serve as the fulcrum for establishing the free trade area by 2010 for the 6 older ASEAN members and 2015 for the 4 newer members [Press Statement by the ASEAN–China Summit, November 4, 2002]. In addition, this time China proposed even a China–Japan–Korea FTA to Japanese and Korean leaders, while the Japanese could not afford to receive the proposal, except as a long-term objective. China at present has signed the FTA with Hong Kong, which has in turn initiated talks with New Zealand and has been approached by Singapore. [NKS, April 12, 2002].

Japan and China are competing for access to ASEAN, and in the end, the two countries are likely to become involved in region-wide East Asian economic cooperation or economic integration drive. This fact is of crucial importance.

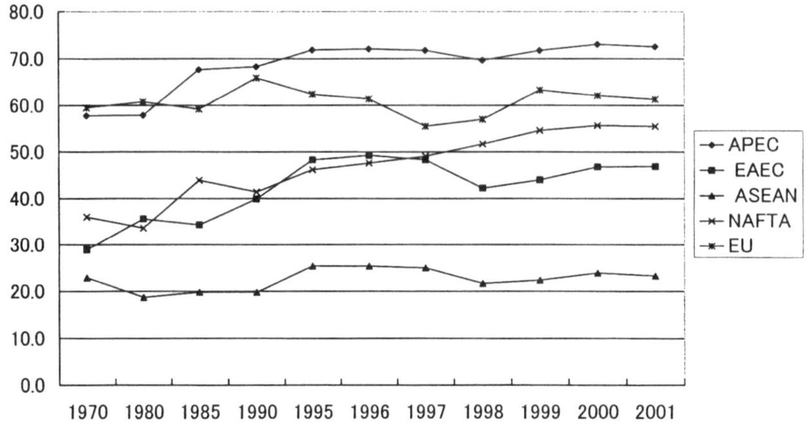

Fig. 2. Intraregional export rates of trade blocs, 1970–2001. Source: World Bank 2003

5. The Political Economy of Regional Cooperation in East Asia

5.1 Regional Integration in East Asia and Japan's Problems

The impact of the currency crisis and the currency union in Europe taught East Asia lessons on how best to cope with globalization. Monetary cooperation and economic integration through FTAs are two main pillars of the effort to move toward greater East Asian economic cooperation. This brought the creation of the ASEAN+3 regional framework and the vision of an "East Asian community." Newly industrializing countries in East Asia, such as Malaysia, Singapore, Korea, and Thailand, are strongly conscious of the need for such cooperation. For them, the merits and demerits of globalization are clear.

What kind of obstacles are there on the path to further progress for regional integration? Figure 2 shows the intraregional export rate of economic blocs. The regional export rate of APEC is the highest at about 70%, 10% higher than that of the European Union. The APEC region can be recognized as having three main subregions: NAFTA, EAEC, and ASEAN. NAFTA's intraregional export share increased from 36% in 1970 to 55% in 1999, while the share of EAEC rose from 29% to 44% but fell after the crisis. By contrast, ASEAN's share has remained stagnant at about 20%. It is therefore possible to view the APEC region as consisting of two parts. Increasing the intraregional export share of these two subregions has caused an increase in the APEC share.

Figure 3 shows the trade balances of the main economies related to East Asia in 1985 and 2001. Japan's export balances are all in surplus except with China, and its surplus is increasing steadily. The United States and China are contrasted with Japan. The United States increased deficits with all trade partners and the deficit has

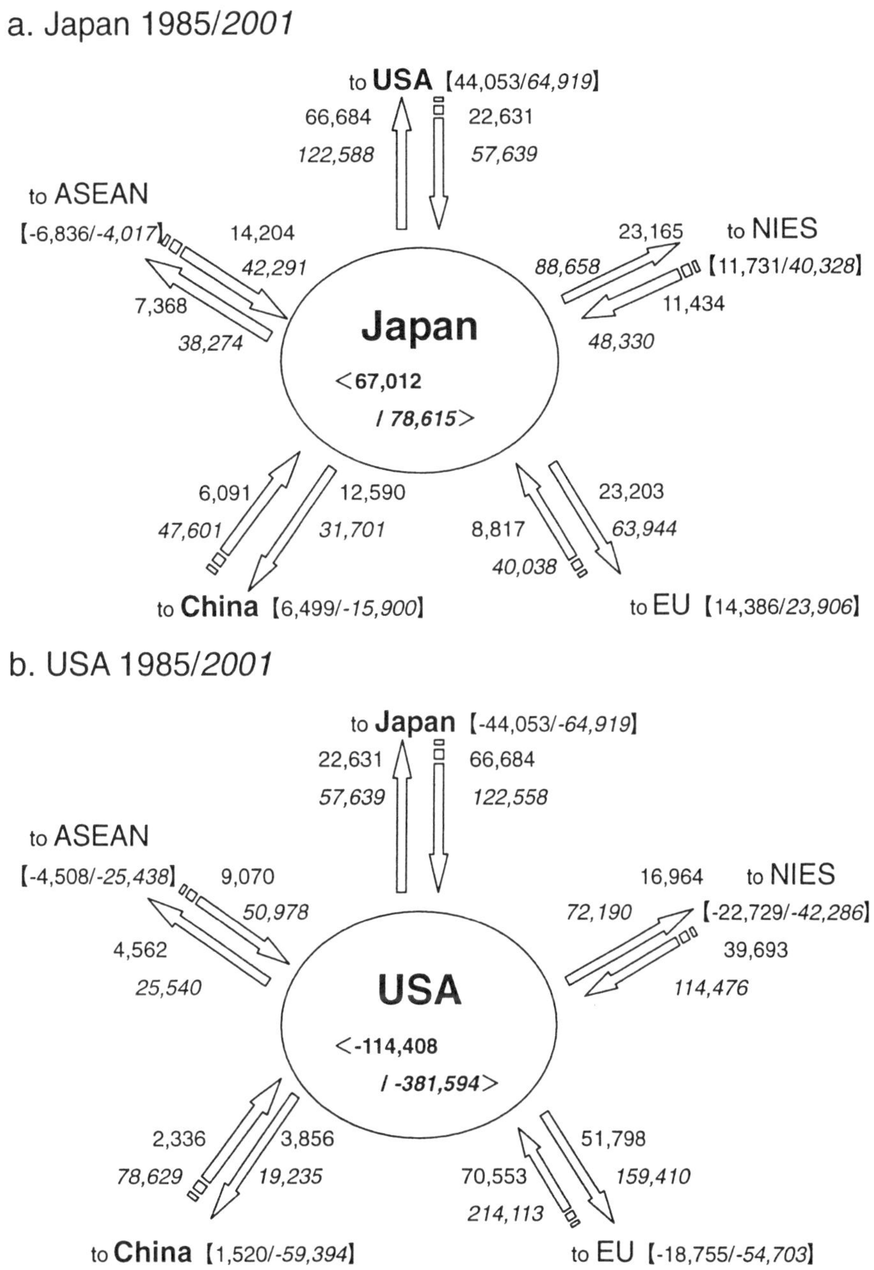

Fig. 3. Trade balance of major countries/regions related to East Asia (by region, 1985 and 2001). Source: JETRO World Trade Matrix (www.jetro.go.jp/ec/j/trade/excel/matrix2001.xls)

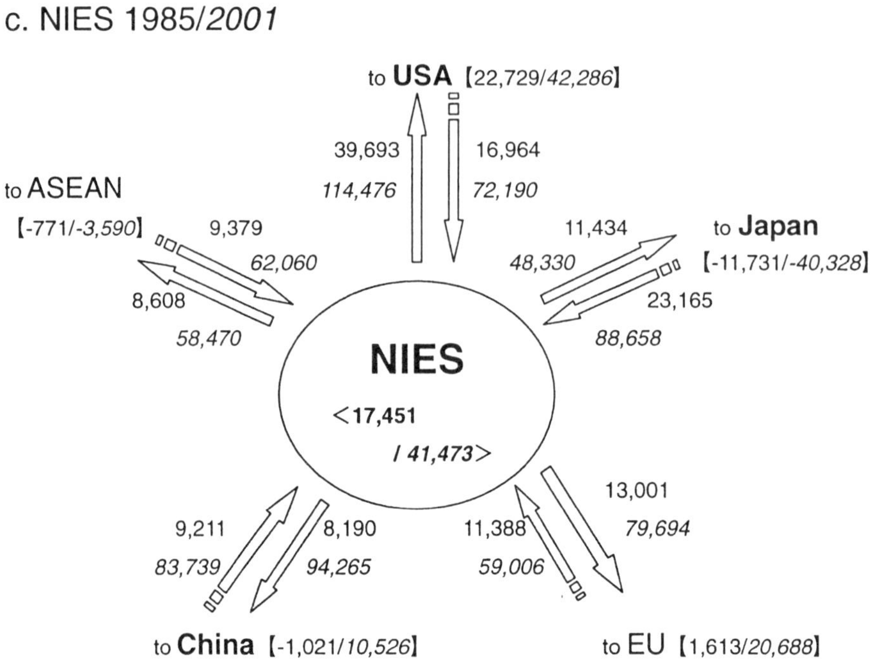

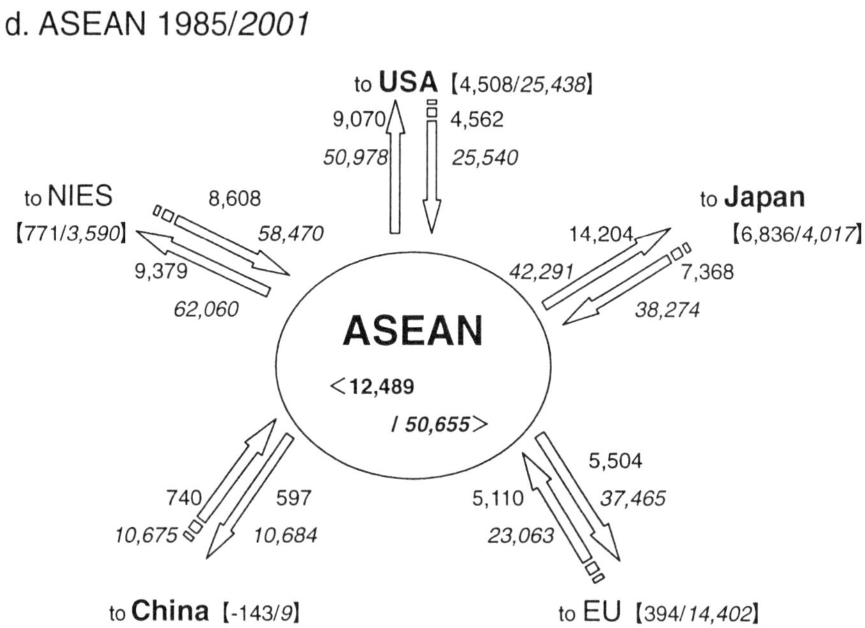

Fig. 3. *Continued*

e. China 1985/*2001*

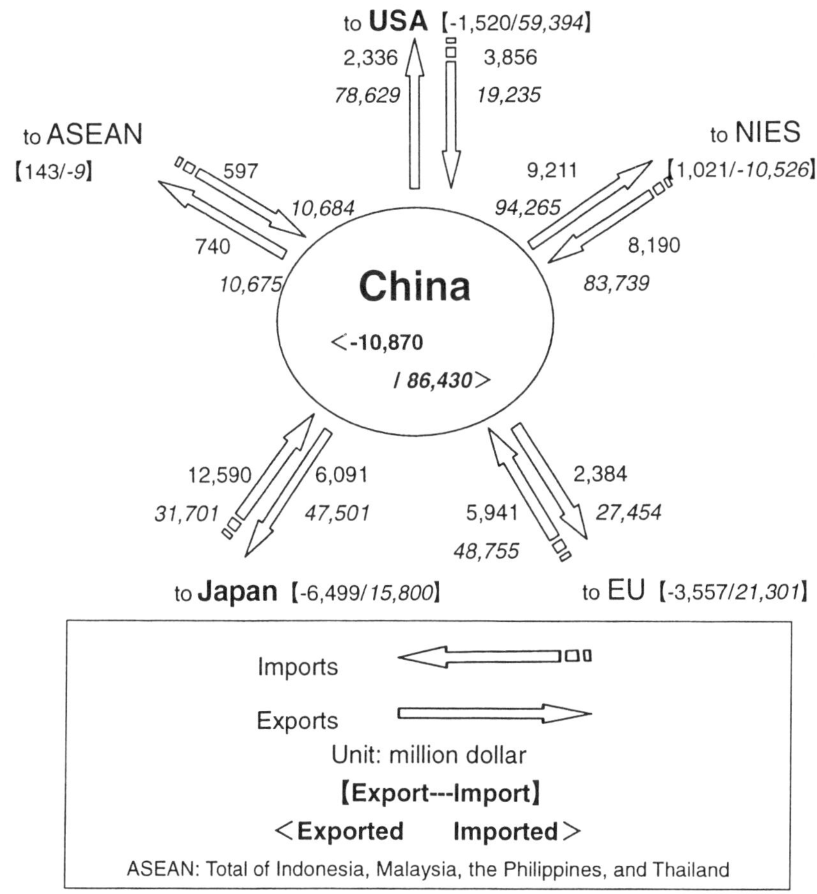

Fig. 3. *Continued*

become huge. Its total trade balance came to $382 billion in 2001, while China has a large surplus with the United States but deficits with ASEAN and the newly industrializing economies (NIEs), which means that China may be playing the role of an absorber of goods. The abnormal and continuous trade deficits of the United States suggest a lack of sustainability and/or instability of the United States market and an excessive dependence on the part of East Asia on American markets. One means of reducing this excessive dependence is the opening of the Japanese market to East Asia. If the present trade structure continues, the Japanese economic position will decline because of the increasing significance of the Chinese market. Therefore, Japanese political influence in East Asia will decline as well. Instead, China's economic and political presence will increase.

Considering East Asia's balanced growth, the Japanese role is very important. Japan has been able to supply capital, technology, management skills, and other contributions to East Asian countries. Now, Japan should open her economy to East Asia. This will, in turn, create a favorable cycle of development within East Asia. Japan must assist in achieving balanced economic growth in the region. This is a precondition for Japan itself to develop further.

In fact, many Japanese manufacturing firms have shifted their production sites to NIEs, ASEAN member countries, and China. The development of the international division of labor is decisive for Japanese firms to maintain their competitiveness in the world market. In August and September 1999, the Mission for Revitalization of the Asian Economy, headed by Hiroshi Okuda, Chairman of the Board of the Toyota Motor Corporation and Chairman of the Japan Federation of Employers' Association (Nikkeiren), visited the main East Asian countries and made a report in which it was stated that East Asia is a "community with a common fate." The report stated that "the currency crisis hit many Asian countries almost simultaneously. This is an indication that the countries of Asia are developing into a community. No longer just a collection of individual countries, their economic and social ties are growing stronger" [Mission 1999]. In July 2000, another major business association, the Japan Federation of Economic Organizations (Keidanren), which merged with Nikkeiren in May 2002, made a proposal titled "Urgent Call for Active Promotion of Free Trade Agreements," in which the main reasons for promoting FTAs were summarized. Priority regions for Japan's FTA policy were East Asia and the Americas, in that order. The Keidanren also urged, in a report entitled "Towards the Implementation of Strategic Trade Policies: A Grand Design of Japan's Policy as a Nation Built on Trade," that "the East Asian region, centered on ASEAN, China, and the of Korea, is gaining prominence as the most important base for global operations of Japanese businesses," and "creating common business infrastructure in East Asia and thereby linking related business networks would lead to maintaining an increase in the competitiveness of the entire East Asia region in addition to maintaining and increasing the competitive advantage of Japanese companies" [Keidanren 2001].

In spite of these initiatives, Japan has been swinging between the United States and East Asia, and it is distrusted by East Asian countries and their people. An article entitled "East Asia's Puzzling Regionalism" in the *Far Eastern Economic Review* [Dieter 2001] depicted the Chiang Mai Initiative, in May 2000, as follows: "The Chiang Mai initiative could have been the first step of monetary integration in East Asia, eventually leading to a monetary union.…At this initiative, the relevant bilateral agreements have been linked to the consent of the International Monetary Fund for drawing down major parts of credit lines. For example, if a country needs to draw more than 10% of its agreed credit facility with the Japanese central bank, it needs IMF approval.…This is puzzling." The article goes on to say, "Paradoxically, Japan appears to be both the driving force for monetary regionalism in East Asia and its main opponent. Japan wants to lead the region, but it is only able to supply hollow leadership. Rather than providing the framework for genuine and deep integration, Japan wishes to maintain its status in the region, while at the same time not provoking criticism in Washington. Such ambivalence, being neither a part of the West nor a widely accepted player in Asia, might have worked in the past. Today, Japan's approach to regionalism, characterized by its preference for hierarchy and its negligence of neighbors' demands, won't work. And, absent Japanese leadership,

China, in the medium term, may be able to fill that vacuum" [Dieter 2001: 29]. Here it was again pointed out that Japan may be replaced by China for failing to take a leadership role.

In Europe and the Americas, economic integration progresses and the cause of currency union also advances. East Asia is not an exception. Economic integration is important. As economic ties beyond national borders improve, currency stability is needed more than ever to safeguard further development. This is a way for Japan to strengthen its competitiveness.

The reasons for Japan's hesitancy include its view of Asia, political pressure from the United States and political opposition at home to liberalization of trade in agricultural products. Japan is no longer the only advanced or developed country in East Asia. Political leadership is now gradually diffusing to other East Asian countries. Japan's view should change from the outlook of the past to the view of the future with a common goal of an "East Asian community."

There is a deep-rooted fear in Japan that China poses a threat. Japan may lose economic and political influence as China becomes more important, but this does not necessarily have to take place. The Japanese people, especially politicians, realize that the Japanese economy already has very strong ties with China, and many realize that strengthening these ties would benefit both countries.

As the Okuda Mission to Asia made clear, Japan and East Asia share a common destiny. In the framework of East Asia as a whole, Japan and perhaps China should put their future into a common East Asian society, considering seriously the ASEAN/Korea initiative. If so, relations between Japan and the United States will change. This problem is very serious for other East Asian countries as well as Japan and will be discussed in more detail in the next section.

5.2 Other Problems of Economic Integration in East Asia

Needless to say, economic integration does not bring benefits to all member countries and industries. Until recently, some ASEAN members were critical of Singapore's attempt to form FTAs with countries outside ASEAN. Malaysia and Indonesia accused Singapore of undermining ASEAN unity. According to their criticism, any of Singapore's FTA partners could export their products to the AFTA market with preferential tariffs. The FTAs are a kind of a "backdoor entry" for non-ASEAN members. Therefore, Singapore pursues a selfish, "go-it-alone" strategy, which does damage to the development of other ASEAN members [Mahathir 2001: 33; *Straits Times* online, May 3 and 10, 2001; Rajan et al. 2001: 77]. In fact, Malaysia has decided to postpone tariff reduction on automobile parts by three years in order to protect domestic industries against imports from abroad. It is a serious issue for countries with less competitiveness to liberalize their markets rapidly. In reply to such criticism, the Singaporean government explained that ASEAN had a system to ensure compliance to a "rule of origin" condition, whereby at least 40% of a product's content must originate from within ASEAN for it to enjoy AFTA's preferential treatment [*Straits Times* online, May 3 and 10, 2001].

It is very important for ASEAN+3 to try to narrow the gap between rich and poor. In this regard, the Initiative for ASEAN Integration (IAI) seems important. At the Fourth ASEAN Informal Summit in November 2000, leaders agreed to launch the IAI. Its aim is to narrow the divide within ASEAN and enhance ASEAN competitiveness as a region. Under the IAI, Singapore offered to set up, under a five-year technical assistance program, several training institutes in Cambodia, Laos, Myanmar, and Vietnam, to provide information technology (IT) "train-the trainers" courses and training attachments to educational institutions. China, Japan, and Korea all supported the IAI. They also agreed to work toward an "Asian IT belt" to link cities of IT excellence in Asia. In addition, China announced an increased contribution to the ASEAN–China Cooperation Fund [Fourth ASEAN Summit Chairman 2000]. A social safety net is also provided for the poor.

China's accession to the WTO was realized in November 2001 after 15 years of negotiations. The impact of China, with its 1.3 billion people, on other East Asian countries is huge. JETRO's White Paper 2001 views the effects of China's accession to the WTO as follows: "China and the ASEAN region will increasingly compete with each other for foreign capital. This will require the ASEAN members to further integrate their regional market of 500 million people. They will also have to improve their economic efficiency." This increase in efficiency, suggests the white paper, should be brought about by gradually scrapping internal tariff and nontariffs barriers as required by the ASEAN Free Trade Area (AFTA) schedule; strengthening and encouraging the agglomeration of supplier ["supporting"] industries; enhancing their physical and services infrastructure for more efficient movement of people, goods, and funds within the region; and pursuing the further internationalization and transparency of business rules governing trade, investment and business in general [JETRO 2001c: 29].

There is also a Chinese threat in the ASEAN region. However, as noted above for Japan, this only makes the achievement of East Asian unity more pressing. Economic ties are very strong. Symbiosis should be the basis of talks from the very beginning. In fact, as indicated by the JETRO White Paper, ASEAN competes with China in attracting foreign investment capital. However, trade between the two regions is steadily increasing.

It is worth noting the results of JETRO's recent survey of business operations. According to a survey of 2,567 JETRO members conducted in October 2001 (720 firms participating with a response rate of 28%), the share of Japanese firms expecting to invest in China in the following three years was greater than the share planning to invest elsewhere in the region at 96%, followed by ASEAN-bound investment plans at 68%, Asian NIEs at 51%, Europe at 49%, and the United States at 40%. On the question of whether firms now operating abroad were aiming to continue their overseas operations or not, 99% of firms responded that they expected to continue operations at their present sites. The share of firms expecting divestment was only 2%. Reasons given for a continuing presence in a given region were in particular "enlargement of AFTA market" (32%), "levels of past investment" (31%), "avoidance of risk of investment concentration in China" (29%) and "enough ASEAN-based operations" (28%) [JETRO 2001d]. In short, not all Japanese firms rush to invest in China. In general, mutual economic integration seems to be progressing.

The relation between regional cooperation or regionalism in East Asia and the United States must be taken into account. Both Mahathir's proposal for an EAEG and the Japanese government's AMF proposal faced strong opposition from the United States. The Miyazawa Initiative and the Chiang Mai Initiative were carefully worded so as to avoid opposition from the United States.[22] The stance of the United States toward increased integration in East Asia presents an obstacle to stronger regional cooperation in the areas of trade and finance.

The United States has often responded in an irrational manner to the trade initiatives of other nations or regions, at least when these initiatives do not involve the United States. This was true in the case of the European Union. Fred Bergsten, director of the Institute for International Economics, has pointed out that even if European proposals were constructive, the United States officials opposed them simply because they were not being carried out at the initiative of the United States. He calls the behavior of his own country "schizophrenic" [Bergsten 1999: 30–31]. The United States' attitude toward East Asia could be more severe than in the European case. Especially since the terrorist attacks of September 11, American unilateralism has become much stronger. Even though the United States has become more selfish, East Asians have to insist on the necessity of regional cooperation. East Asians need to fit East Asian regionalism into the world economy. For East Asia, the parallel frameworks of APEC and ASEAN+3 are needed as supplements to each other.

Three FTA characteristics detailed in a World Bank summary, are particularly interesting. The first one is so-called "deep integration," which "requires more than reducing tariffs and quotas." The typical case is the "Single Market Program of the European Union." The second one is not "closed regionalism," but a more outward-looking construction, in other words, "open regionalism." The third characteristic is the "equal partner" model between advanced countries and developing countries [World Bank 2000: 1–2]. East Asia's economic integration cannot be of the "closed regionalism" type that was prevalent among developing countries adopting an import substitution strategy in the 1960s and 1970s, but should rather be a form of "open regionalism." East Asia has developed through triangular trade, and the American market was and will continue to be the single largest market for some time. East Asia's regionalism and financial cooperation should not be fostered through protection from imports from abroad. Through regional integration, East Asia will develop a regional economy and "community." Therefore, one should not conceive of the world economy as divided into the three blocs of Europe, the Americas, and East Asia as the outcome of protectionism, but rather as three separate units serving to create a more balanced economy in the process of globalization.

Finally, a stronger East Asian community will come about through trust among the region's countries and peoples. In this respect, nongovernmental organizations are new actors that facilitate the interchange of people and possess the power to influence state policies. Their role must increase substantially in the future. They have the potential to create a new East Asian society from the ground up.

References

ADB [Asian Development Bank] (1999) Asian development outlook 1999. Oxford University Press, New York

APEC (1997) 1997 Result report: Message from the chair of APEC 1997 (November 23)

ASEAN Secretariat (1995) ASEAN: An overview. ASEAN, Jakarta

ASEAN+3 Summit (1999) Joint statement on East Asian cooperation. Manila (November 28)

ASEAN+3 Summit (2001) Press statement by the chairman of the 7th ASEAN summit and the 5th ASEAN+3 summit. Bangar Seri Begawan (November 5)

Bhagwati J, Greenaway D, Panagariya A (1998) Trading preferentially: theory and policy. Economic Journal 108 (July)

Baldwin RE (1997) The causes of regionalism. World Economy 20

Bergsten CF (1998) Reviving the Asian monetary fund. International Economics Policy Briefs 98-8 (December)

Bergsten CF (1999) America and Europe: clash of the titans. Foreign Affairs 78: 2 (March/April)

BIS (1999) Banks' interactions with highly leveraged institutions. Bank for International Settlements, Basel (January)

BIS (2000) Banks' interactions with highly leveraged institutions: Implementation of the Basle committee's sound practices paper. Bank for International Settlements, Basel (January)

Chaipravat O (2001) Towards a regional financing arrangement in East Asia. Paper presented at ADBI/FIMA symposium on "From the Asian financial crisis of 1997 to a regional financing agreement", Honolulu (May 10)

Council [Council on foreign exchange and other transactions] (1999) Internationalization of the yen for the 21st century: Japan's response to changes in global economic and financial environments. Ministry of Finance, Tokyo (April 20)

Dieter H (2001) East Asia's puzzling regionalism. Far Eastern Economic Review (July 12)

EAVG [East Asia Vision Group] (2001) Towards an East Asian community: region of peace, prosperity and progress. Report submitted to the ASEAN+ 3 Leaders (October 31)

Eichengreen B (1994) International monetary arrangements for the 21st century. Brookings Institution, Washington DC (Japanese translation 1997)

FEER (1999) Asia 1999 Yearbook. Far Eastern Economic Review, Hong Kong

Fourth ASEAN Summit Chairman (2000) Press statement by chairman, 4th ASEAN informal summit. Singapore (November 25)

Funabashi Y (2002) Point of view: new geopolitics rages over various parts of Asia. *Asahi Shimbun* newspaper (January 15)

G-7 Finance Ministers (1999) Report of G-7 Finance Ministers to the economic summit. Cologne (June)

Hirakawa H (1999) East Asia's currency and economic crisis and a new financial and cooperation order: a view from Japan. Paper presented at the Global Forum, Taegu, Korea (October 6–8, 1999)

Hirakawa H (2001) East Asia's currency and economic crisis and the development of regional cooperation. Economic Research Center Discussion Paper 130, Graduate School of Economics, Nagoya University

Hirakawa H (2002) Ajia tsuuka kiki: Tonan Ajia heno inpakuto" [East Asia's currency crisis: impact on Southeast Asia). In: Suehiro A (Ed) Iwanami kouza tonan ajia shi: Dai kyu kan (Series of the history of Southeast Asia) 9. Iwanami Shoten, Tokyo

IMF [International Monetary Fund] (1998) An answer of Mr. Stanley Fischer. IMF seminar on capital account liberalization, Washington DC (March 10)

IMF (1999a) IMF's response to the Asian crisis. IMF, Washington DC (January)
IMF (1999b) IMF concludes article IV consultation with Malaysia. IMF, Washington DC (September 8)
JETRO (2001a) Reference materials of JETRO international symposium "Prospects of regional economic integration in Asia." JETRO, Tokyo (March 1)
JETRO (2001b) FTA sanko shiryo (FTA reference materials). JETRO, Tokyo (July)
JETRO (2001c) JETRO White Paper on international trade 2001 (Summary). JETRO, Tokyo
JETRO (2001d) Press release: Nobiga donkashita sekaino chokusetsutoushi (White Paper on foreign direct investment 2002: World foreign direct investment which slowed down the rate of increase). JETRO, Tokyo
Jin NG (2000) Coping with the Asian financial crisis: the Singapore experience. ISEAS Working Paper, Visiting Researchers Series 8. Institute of Southeast Asian Studies, Singapore
Keidanren [Japan Federation of Economic Organization] (2000) Urgent call for active promotion of Free Trade Agreements: towards a new dimension in trade policy. Keidanren, Tokyo (July 18)
Keidanren (2001) Towards the implementation of strategic trade policies: a grand design of Japan's policy as a nation built on trade. Keidanren, Tokyo (June)
Köhler H (2001) New challenge for exchange rate policy. Remarks at the ASEM [Asia-Europe Meeting] of Finance Ministers, Kobe (January 13)
Madhur S (2001) Costs and benefits of a common currency for the ASEAN. Paper presented at international conference "Monetary outlook on East Asia in an integrating world economy." Chulalongkorn University, Bangkok (September 5–6)
Mahathir M (2001) Shimpojumu deno Mahatiiru no Kaitou (An answer to the question at symposium "Beyond globalism and globalization"). Nihon Keizai Shimbunsha, Tokyo
METI (2000) White paper on international trade 2000. Ministry of Economy, Trade and Industry, Tokyo
METI (2001) White paper on international trade 2001. Ministry of Economy, Trade and Industry, Tokyo (May)
Mission (1999) Report of the mission for revitalization of the Asian economy: living in harmony with Asia in the twenty-first century. Ministry of Foreign Affairs, Tokyo (November)
Miyazawa K (1998) Statement by the Hon. Kiichi Miyazawa, Minister of Finance of Japan at the fifty-third joint annual discussion, delivered by the Hon. Sadakazu Tanigaki, State Secretary of Finance (October 6)
Miyazawa K (1999) Statement by Finance Minister Kiichi Miyazawa. Ministry of Finance, Tokyo (January 1) [Ministry of Finance homepage: www.mof.go.jp/english/if/e1e060.htm]
Moon W, Rhee Y, Yoon DR (2000) Asian monetary cooperation: a search for regional monetary stability in the post-euro and the post-Asian crisis era. Economic Papers 3: 1 (May). Bank of Korea, Seoul
Mukoyama H (2001) Changes in Korea's international economic relations in the 1990s. RIM 2: 2. Japan Research Institute, Economics Department Center for Pacific Business Studies, Tokyo
Pempel TJ (1999) Conclusion. In: Pempel TJ (Ed) The politics of the Asian economic crisis. Cornell University Press, Ithaca
Rajan RS, Sen R, Siregar R (2001) Singapore and free trade agreements: economic relations with Japan and the United States. Institute of Southeast Asian Studies, Singapore
Ramangkura V (1999) Cooperation for conquering crisis in East Asia. Paper presented at JETRO international symposium "Merits and demerits of globalization and the future of Asia." JETRO, Tokyo (February)

Scollay R, Gilbert JP (2001) New regional trading arrangements in the Asia Pacific. Institute of International Economics, Washington DC (May)

Shinohara, H (1999) Chiikikyoryoku to shiteno ajia tsuka kiko (An Asian monetary organization as regional cooperation). The Japan Center for Economic Research Bulletin, 836 (December 1)

Sucharithanarugse W (1998) Impacts of Asian financial crisis on Thai economy and the implementation of AFTA. Paper presented at the international workshop on "AFTA and Asian economies in perspective of the Asian financial crisis." Hanoi (February 26–27)

Supachai P (2001) Atarashii jiyu bouekiken no arikatawo teisho shitai (I would like to propose what a new free trade zone should be). In: Nihon Keizai Shimbunsha (Ed) Ajia chiikitogo heno mosaku (Groping for East Asian regional integration). Nihon Keizai Shimbunsha, Tokyo

Syed OA (1992) EAEC & AFTA: Eventuality out of necessity [http://vlib.unitarklj1.edu.my/staff-publications/datuk/EAEC.pdf] (December 24)

UNCTAD (1996) Handbook of economic integration and cooperation groupings of developing countries, Vol. 1 – Regional and subregional economic integration groupings, United Nations, New York

UNCTAD (2001) Trade and development report, 2001. United Nations, New York

Vichyanond P (2000) Do we need a regional lender of last resort? In: Vichyanond P et al. (Eds) Regional financial cooperation. Thailand Development Research Institute Foundation, Bangkok

Yam JCK (1997) Asian monetary cooperation: The Per Jacobsson lecture. SAR Hong Kong Association of Banks, Hong Kong

Yoshitomi M (2001) Ajia kyotsuu tsuuka no jitsugen mo yume dewanai (An Asian common currency would not be a dream). In: Nihon Keizai Shimbunsha (Ed) Ajia chiikitogo heno mosaku (Groping for East Asian regional integration). Nihon Keizai Shimbunsha, Tokyo

World Bank (2000) Trade blocs. Oxford University Press, New York

World Bank (2001) World development indicators 2001. World Bank, Washington DC

Notes

[1] Short-term external debt in the countries affected by currency crisis generally exceeded international reserves immediately before the crisis. Short-term external debt–international reserve ratios in second quarter of 1997 were 1.45 in Thailand, 1.70 in Indonesia, 2.06 in Korea, and 0.61 in Malaysia. Singapore was the highest at 2.44 [ADB 1999: 26]. Nevertheless, Singapore could contain the contagion effects of the crisis. According to the explanation of Ngiam Kee Jin of the National University of Singapore, Singapore weathered the crisis better than most East Asian countries because "Singapore has built three strong foundations in the form of strong fundamentals, a flexible exchange rate system, and an adjustable wage system, which would be sufficient to ensure its resilience against any currency crises." However, he also pointed out that there were its regulations. "To ensure that its regulations were not being circumvented through financial derivatives, the Monetary Authority of Singapore (MAS) has defined Singapore dollar credit facilities to include a wide range of financial instruments, including foreign exchange swaps, currency swaps, interest rate swaps, facilities incorporating options, and forward rate agreements in Singapore dollars' [Jin 2000: 11 and 20].

[2] The IMF said, "Directors broadly agreed that the regime of capital control—which was intended by the authorities to be temporary—had produced more positive results than many

observers had initially expected" [IMF 1999b].

3 The EMEAP official home page (http://www.emeap.org:8084) gives a brief history of the EMEAP during both an initial period, from 1991 to 1996, and a second period from 1996 to the present, following the establishment of Governors' Meeting and working/study groups.

4 An article in the *Japan Center for Economic Research Bulletin* mentioned one reason why the Japanese government could promptly respond to some ASEAN countries' request and take positive action by proposing an Asian Monetary Fund (AMF). According to this article, one concerned authority and some institute researchers had already started studying something like an AMF in the autumn of 1996. They had thought that even though monetary crisis in a certain East Asian developing country would, like the 1994 Mexican crisis, stand out, the United States and the IMF would not provide serious timely help to the East Asian country as they did in the case of Mexico. However, East Asian countries together have enough money to cope with the crisis in terms of foreign reserves, so East Asian countries should build a framework for the region to deal with such crises. Therefore, the Japanese government's idea of an AMF was being contemplated to some extent by the beginning of 1997 [Shinohara 1999: 6].

5 The report said elsewhere that, "taking into account recent developments, such as the experiences from the currency crises in the Asian countries with whom Japan maintains close economic ties, and the emergence of the euro, it should be made clear that the internationalization of the yen can contribute to achieving currency and economic stability in the Asian region, as well as throughout the world. Furthermore, it should be realized that this in turn will provide greater stability to the Japanese economy and will promote the national interests of Japan" [Council 1999].

6 The *Asahi Shimbun* newspaper reported that at the ASEAN+3 summit meeting held in Singapore in November 2000, China strongly opposed use of the yen as a reserve currency in ASEAN+3 swap arrangements. One article stated that "the internationalization of the yen should never be put forward and that China maintains a strong rejection of the yen bloc on the one hand while on the other she is trying to become a hard currency country [*Asahi Shimbun* newspaper, November 11, 2000].

7 At an international conference of the *Nihon Keizai Shimbun* newspaper, held in June 2001, the Dean of the Asian Development Bank Institute, Masaru Yoshitomi, set forth his views on the crisis in East Asia. According to him, the crisis in East Asia was not a current account crisis but a capital flight crisis and a crisis which drastic outflows of the dollar gave rise to. It is natural that relief should be provided by a regional organization. "Its role is like [that of] the central bank, which supplies liquidity to a bank affected by crisis, when a domestic bank falls into liquidity crisis. Internationally the IMF is expected to play the role of lender of last resort. However, the IMF is not the central bank in such a sense. If not, who performs the role? It is unthinkable but that only a regional lender of last resort who performs it. If the crisis takes place in Mexico, the United States may extend a helping hand to her. Taking into account regional politics, it is logically natural that in each region, a regional lender of last resort comes into being" [Yoshitomi 2001: 128–129].

8 An article in *Asiaweek* on the Chiang Mai Initiative states: "Trying to head off another 1997-style Crisis, they [ASEAN+3 countries] came up with something officially dubbed the Chiang Mai Initiative, which people are already calling the 'Asian Monetary Fund'." [http://www.asiaweek.com/asiaweek/ A New Currency Frontline? March 15, 2000].

9 The World Trade Organization (WTO) defines regionalism as "actions by governments to liberalize or facilitate trade on a regional basis, sometimes through free-trade areas or customs unions". In the WTO context, regional trade agreements (RTAs) have both a more general and a more specific meaning: more general, because RTAs may be agreements concluded between countries not necessarily belonging to the same geographical region; more specifically, because the provisions of GATT Article XXIV and Article V of the General Agreement on Trade in Services (GATS) relate specifically to conditions of preferen-

tial trade liberalization with RTAs." [http://www.wto.org]. According to the WTO, regionalism means regional trade agreement. However, in this chapter, RTAs—that is, free trade agreements [FTAs]—are considered to be a main reflection of "regionalism," thus the term is used in a broader sense.

10 The 12 EU countries adopting the euro are Germany, France, Italy, Spain, Belgium, Luxembourg, the Netherlands, Austria, Portugal, Finland, Ireland, and Greece.

11 As to critics, the Deputy Secretary General of the Institute of Islamic Understanding Malaysia, Syed Othaman Alhabshi brought a counterargument: "The main criticism is that it is an attempt to create a closed trade bloc; an attempt to 'draw a line' down the Pacific and to divide the Pacific; racist, exclusivist, and exclusionary; and an attempt to destroy or undermine APEC. How could it create a closed trade bloc when such a stance would be completely against the policies of each participation country? If EAEC would divide the Asia-Pacific region, how about NAFTA, Australia, and New Zealand Closer Economic Relations, etc.? To allege that EAEC is racist is simply beyond comprehension" [Syed 1992].

12 Prime Minister Hashimoto visited Brunei, Malaysia, Indonesia, Vietnam, and Singapore in January 1997.

13 Columbia University Professor Jagdish Bhagwati has called this the "spaghetti bowl" phenomenon. It is the "phenomenon of numerous and crisscrossing PTAs [his term for FTAs] and innumerable applicable tariff rates depending on arbitrarily determined and often a multiplicity of source of origin." His conclusion is as follows: "In the guise of freeing trade, PTAs have managed to re-create the preferences-ridden world of the 1930s as surely as protectionism did at the time. Irony, indeed!" [Bagwati et al. 1998: 1139]. Paul Krugman is also skeptical about FTAs. According to him, it is the worst outcome if the world divides into three trade zones: Europe, the western hemisphere, and East Asia. Scollay and Gilbert share this opinion [Scollay and Gilbert 2001: 6]. By contrast, R.E. Baldwin analyzed Krugman's explanation of why regionalism is easier and other standard explanations of regionalism. He advocates a domino theory of regionalism. As for discrimination against nonmember countries, he concluded that "trade is already quite free in the major trading nations, few regional liberalizations are capable of creating important antiliberalization forces [the exceptions are likely to be South–South FTAs]" [Baldwin 1997: 877–883, 886]. The World Bank accepted FTAs on a realistic basis. The Bank pointed out that most of the arguments are political. "It is rather reasonable to treat the effects of such schemes as being additional to whatever unilateral and global liberalization might be underway. This is our approach. However, the poor should not be denied the association rights already conferred by both the United States and the EU on several middle-income countries" [World Bank 2000: 124, 132; see also JETRO 2001b].

14 ASEAN said that "aside from influencing intraregional trading activities, the primary objective of AFTA is to promote greater foreign direct investment and intra-ASEAN investment in the region. Another important aim of AFTA is to promote ASEAN as a competitive production base geared towards serving the global market" [ASEAN Secretariat 1995: 12].

15 The White Paper on International Trade of the Japanese Ministry of Economy, Trade and Industry pointed to a recent surge of the number of FTAs characterized as the "conclusion of agreements aimed at establishing de facto standards for trade rules," and that the EU, Singapore, Mexico, Chile, and other countries have made such a strategy [METI 2001: 199].

16 Regarding a Japan–Korea Free Trade Agreement, it was mentioned that the Japanese Ambassador to Korea, Kazuo Ogura, already had proposed an FTA to the Korean government in September 1998 [Mukoyama 2001: 61]. However it would be a mistake to consider his remark as an informal proposal from the Japanese government. As is well known, there was and still is a strong opposition against the liberalization of agricultural products in Japanese domestic politics. Such a proposal from the Japanese government in that situation is unthinkable. If such a remark was made, it seems to have been a strictly personal opinion.

[17] The official title is The Agreement between Japan and the Republic of Singapore for a New-Age Economic Partnership (JSEPA).

[18] In 1997, at the APEC meeting in Vancouver, the EVSL initiative was proposed, targeting 15 sectors for early liberalization.

[19] *The Japan Times* made some interesting comments on an East Asia free trade zone. "ASEAN is eager to enhance economic ties with Japan in the face of intensifying competition from China, whose low-cost labor attracts Japanese companies, contributing to its rapid export-driven economic expansion" and "The Japan–ASEAN framework is also aimed at countering the recent move by China to conclude, for its part, an FTA with ASEAN, the sources said." [*Japan Times* online, April 29, 2001: www.japantimes.co.jp/cgi-bin/getarticle.pl5?nn20010429a3.htm].

[20] The NKS said, although Japan gave a joint antiterrorism statement top priority at the summit, "Japan's intention of showing her existence in diplomacy and sharing the role with the United States in terms with the antiterrorism appeared to be rejected by ASEAN and China" [NKS, November 6, 2001].

[21] The *Asahi Shimbun* newspaper wrote: "During its summit meeting that opens Monday in Brunei, the ASEAN is expected to formally agree on a goal to conclude a free trade agreement with China within 10 years, according to Thai government sources." In order to persuade them to start to study the FTA between the two, "China told ASEAN members that a free trade area would never come into being in East Asia if they wait for Japan and South Korea to join" [asahi.com, November 3, 2001].

[22] An article in *Asiaweek* explains the relation of the United States and the Chiang Mai Initiative: "Some Americans, who hated this sort of thing in the past, concede it might not be a bad idea. Maybe that's because all the participants in the discussion took care to word the proposal in ways that wouldn't offend Washington. Eisuke Sakakibara, a former Japanese vice finance minister for international affairs, is a backer of the scheme. It has a distinct Japanese provenance – even though Finance Minister Kiichi Miyazawa denies any link between the current plan and one bearing his name that emanated from Tokyo in 1997....In his Chiang Mai speech Miyazawa said the magic words to keep the Americans in the audience happy. 'Regional cooperation should be essential in improving regulatory frameworks and accounting systems to ensure greater transparency'." [Asiaweek.com, May 19, 2000]. The Miyazawa Initiative carried the word "new" with it. At the IMF–World Bank annual meeting held in September 1988, Miyazawa made the proposal for resolving the Latin American debt crisis. The United States strongly opposed his proposal and the plan was abandoned. But later, the U.S. Treasury Secretary, Nicholas F. Brady, proposed the "New Debt Strategy," which was similar to the Miyazawa Initiative. The reason for rejecting his proposal was probably that the United States did not want Japanese leadership in solving the debt problems of developing countries [*Asahi Shimbun* newspaper, March 11, 1989; May 30, 1992]. By labeling the Miyazawa plan "new," it could be construed that the Japanese Ministry of Finance wanted to make a second initiative.

3. East Asia and the Reorientation of the World Economy: Building a Regional Institutional Infrastructure

Eisuke Sakakibara

In the wake of the events of September 11, 2001, many people, particularly Americans, argued, that the world would never be the same again. However, as the shock slowly fades, a more sober analysis of the current situation seems to have emerged. It is hard to believe that one incident, however grave, could suddenly change the world. Indeed, September 11 has changed our perception of the world, but this change seems to have been going on since the mid-1990s. The change in perception has occurred particularly among Americans. The terrorist attacks on the World Trade Center and the Pentagon powerfully brought home to Americans that they, too, are vulnerable to direct attack and that the far-flung web of bases the United States maintains around the globe are no longer sufficient for the country's defense. The United States, in other words, recognizes that it is in the same boat as the rest of the world.

The administration of U.S. President George W. Bush performed a breathtaking change of direction in the area of foreign policy after September 11. It turned its back on American unilateralism and shifted to multilateral mode, seeking support for a global coalition against the threat of terrorism. The U.S. mended relations with the United Nations, paid back dues, and hurriedly appointed an ambassador after an eight-month vacancy. Quite suddenly it was listening to its allies. The U.S. toned down rhetoric on the National Missile Defense (NMD) project to obtain the cooperation of Russia's President Vladimir Putin, as well as watering down what had been a strident attitude toward China (People's Republic of China) and lifting sanctions against India and Pakistan while cautiously reestablishing contact with Iran, which it once regarded as a rogue state.

On the other side, Russia dramatically changed its own foreign policy to forge stronger cooperative ties with the United States, opening its air space for U.S. flights to Central Asia and accepting an American presence in Uzbekistan and Tajikistan. President Bush's decision to abandon the Anti-ballistic Missile (ABM) Treaty is a source of worry, but Putin seems determined to pursue the new course he has chosen. China pledged to cooperate with the United States in the fight against terrorism, and the previous American position of treating China as a strategic rival seems to have changed quite considerably.

Whether this global coalition against terrorism, or American multilateralism, is durable or not is debatable. The coalition is more one of convenience than a community of common values and, as such, may be quite fragile and, most probably, fleeting. However, there are some irreversible aspects of ongoing change that need to be noted.

First, the age of international economics, or of global capitalism, seems to be transforming itself into an age of international politics. In other words, we are witnessing the beginning of the end of *Pax Americana*, or global capitalism under American hegemony. True, the United States is still a dominant power in both military and economic terms, but the international governance system that was led by the United States, the G-8 group of leading industrialized countries and other international organizations, such as the International Monetary Fund (IMF) and the World Bank, seems to be in a state of flux. Just as World War I signaled the end of *Pax Britannica*, the new global war against terrorism seems to be the symbolic event that may be seen by historians as the beginning of the end of *Pax Americana*. The newly strengthened role of the United Nations in the political sphere and the substantially weaker role of the G-8 and the IMF in the economic sphere are indications of a more multilateral and decentralized pattern of world governance.

In the economic sphere, two salient points need to be noted. First, regionalization is beginning to shape a new world order. On January 1, 2002, the euro started circulation in 12of the 15 countries of the European Union (EU). The EU is now set to expand to include countries in central and eastern Europe. By 2005, the Free Trade Area of the Americas (FTAA) will be established with 34 countries participating.

In 1999, the EU had a 27% share of world GDP. The FTAA, had it been established at that time, would have had an estimated 38% of world GDP. While the Association of Southeast Asian Nations (ASEAN) accounted for only 1.75%, the addition of China, Japan, and Korea (Republic of Korea) to that grouping, forming ASEAN+3 (ASEAN-Plus-Three, or APT), would raise their combined share to 20% of world GDP.

Contributing to the motivation for stronger regional ties is the difficulty of achieving progress in the larger multilateral configuration. This difficulty is reflected in the failure of the world trade talks in Seattle in 1999 and the slow progress of the Asia-Pacific Economic Cooperation (APEC) forum in accomplishing a broad regional agenda. Although planning for a new round of world trade talks is underway thanks to the accord struck at Doha, Qatar, in November 2001, it should be noted that it took more than seven years to complete the Uruguay Round negotiations. This could be a persuasive argument for pursuing both a regional agenda as well as a multilateral agenda.

We have already begun to see a shift in the economic power of countries like China and India. China's economy has been growing at almost 10% per year since the late 1970s. India is expected to register a 4.4% growth rate in 2002, surpassing the expected ASEAN growth rate of about 3%. China, India, and other Asian countries combined account for more than one-half of the world's population and generate a significant proportion of world savings. They are on the verge of increasing their production and GDP commensurate with their population and savings. In regard to a long-term perspective on world history, this is the reorientation of the world economy from West to East.

China should not be overestimated in the area of technology; in manufacturing, however, China will without doubt emerge as a major force and will fundamentally change the international division of labor. China's impact will be particularly strong in Asia.

The second point to be made is that the East Asian crisis of 1997–98 brought recognition of the imperfections or lack of governance of globalized markets. The Asian miracle, to a significant degree a result of the open and global nature of this region, suddenly turned into the Asian crisis. Not only global institutions, such as the IMF and the World Bank, but also regional organizations, notably ASEAN and APEC, were unable to perform any useful function in containing the contagion of the crisis. Initial prescriptions by the IMF were misguided and may have aggravated the crisis rather than alleviating it. It is not only the policy recommendations made during the crisis, but also those made before the crisis that need to be reexamined. The trend toward deregulation, particularly in international finance, without concurrent strengthening of financial supervision, has exposed many countries in the region to a degree of risk unmanageable by national governments.

International organizations cannot substitute for national governments in managing these new market risks. What is necessary is not to substitute "market" for "government" but to redefine the role of government in view of the rapidly changing international environment. Joseph Stiglitz correctly points out what needs to be done in the future in his book *Rethinking the East Asian Miracle.* He writes:

Just as before they were misled by the chimera of deregulation – they should have asked instead what is the *right* regulatory structure for their current situation – so too in the future, they will have to resist accepting without question the current mantras of the global marketplace of ideas. There will have to be *strengthened* regulation of securities markets and an improved overall legal environment, especially in areas such as corporate governance and bankruptcy. The legal structures will have to comport with international standards, yet be adapted to their own special situations; wholesale borrowing will not work. (Stiglitz 2001: 523)

Policy efforts have to be largely national. However, the question here, in relation to regional cooperation, is whether genuine regional institutions such as the EU would help national governments in Asia to accelerate their efforts in the right direction. Or should we leave these matters to international organizations, such as the IMF and the WTO? I endorse the establishment of genuine regional organizations in Asia, or at least in East Asia, on several grounds.

First, existing international institutions are strongly biased toward market fundamentalism or the neoclassical paradigm, and their past records in international capital and finance are very poor. The establishment of a genuine regional organization could provide a countervailing force and would contribute to the reform of international organizations. Indeed, international organizations are necessary, but healthy competition among international and regional institutions would help to improve their performance.

Second, international organizations, politically dominated by Western countries and staffed largely by Western economists, often lack sufficient knowledge of regional values, cultures, and history and tend to impose their own views or try to

"Westernize" the country or region in question. Indeed, international standards need to be adhered to, but standards should reflect existing diversities of culture and institutions. Regional organizations can supplement global ones effectively in such areas.

Third, as in the case of the EU, necessary structural reforms, such as the ones mentioned by Stiglitz, can be more smoothly and willingly implemented if such reforms are deemed essential for regional integration. There has been increasing resistance to externally imposed reforms. Regional cooperation or integration (even slow integration) is a more effective way to implement reforms.

Fourth, the lack of global governance, such as the lack of a global lender of last resort or global financial regulation, is expected to continue for the foreseeable future. Rather than completely relying on national governance, there seems to be some room for regional governance. In a region like Asia where the diversity is enormous, regional governance is more difficult than in Europe, for example. However, more flexible and more accommodating frameworks for cooperation could be developed.

Fifth, regional integration has been proceeding quickly in Europe and, to a lesser degree, in the Americas, where there are recent signs of an acceleration. Is it politically feasible or desirable for Asia to be as open and global as in the past? Might not Asia be victimized by these two predatory empires in the future, as it was in the nineteenth and twentieth centuries? This is a rather defensive position but it has been a major driving force behind recent moves toward more regional cooperation in Asia.

If we are to establish a genuine regional organization, what kind of organization should it be? Which countries should be members and what issues should be addressed? A survey of existing regional institutions in East Asia seems to indicate ASEAN+3 (APT) may be the existing institution that could develop into a genuine regional organization. In fact, APT could be extended to include Australia and New Zealand as well. The complementary nature of these two economies to those of Japan, Korea, and China may make cooperation and integration more rewarding than if only the APT countries were involved.

In addition to trade, there is clearly a regional interest in international finance, as evidenced by the success of the Chiang Mai Initiative, which could be covered by such an organization. In my view, cooperation and ultimately integration should proceed in trade, foreign direct investment (FDI), and international finance simultaneously as opposed to sequentially. This would be quite different from the process undertaken in the EU.

In late 2001 China and the ASEAN countries agreed to form a free trade area (FTA) within ten years, with some allowance for preferential treatment of less developed ASEAN countries. South Korea and Japan could join this FTA to make it an "APT FTA". Given the diverse nature of the participating countries, the FTA could, and should, have some preferential conditions and exceptions for particular countries and regions, at least in its initial stages. A pragmatic, rather than purist, approach is required here. Parallel and reciprocal FDI agreements should proceed simultaneously with trade liberalization.

In the area of international finance, two major steps should be taken. First, more coordination of foreign exchange policies in order to stabilize the relationship between the region's currencies seems long overdue. If the won–yen rate, yuan–yen rate, and baht–yen rate move within a relatively narrow range, coordinating the foreign exchange policies of these respective countries would contribute to the stability of their economies.

Eventually, cooperation should develop into the formation of an Asian Currency Unit (ACU) with a flexible snake around the central value, similar to the ECU snake. That is, the joint floating of Asian currencies vis-à-vis the U.S. dollar and the euro with a relatively wide band around the central rate. Although the creation of a common currency à la euro may not be feasible in the short run, a flexible, somewhat informal currency union with an ACU should be possible and beneficial. It would enhance and accelerate integration through trade and FDI. Speculative attacks on a currency or currencies are a realistic possibility, but with a wide and flexible band around the central value of any ACU, Asian countries would likely be able to fend off such speculation with the huge volume of their combined foreign reserves, provided an effective coordination of macro policy is accompanied by joint foreign exchange interventions.

The need to jointly defend an ACU with a wide band logically leads to the second step, i.e., the extension of the Chiang Mai Initiative, which pools a part of the foreign reserves of the participating countries and conducts macroeconomic surveillance, to the formation of an Asian Monetary Fund (AMF). Participating countries can conduct joint intervention and coordination of macroeconomic policies with the AMF as secretariat. Articles of the AMF can provide the modality and modus operandi of coordination and intervention.

Let me emphasize that the concrete proposal I have outlined is just one possibility. The process of forming a genuine regional organization should be gradual and pragmatic. As in the case of Chinese national policy, structural reform needs to proceed in conjunction with market opening or liberalization. Moves need to be gradual and simultaneous on all fronts.

In conclusion, let me reiterate that the medium- to long-term trend is the reorientation of the world economy from West to East and that there is a need for Asian countries to build an appropriate institutional infrastructure to complement this change. Establishment of regional mechanisms consistent with existing global institutions seems to be the best strategy to pursue, at least for the foreseeable future.

References

Stiglitz J (2001) From miracle to crisis to recovery: lessons from four decades of East Asian experience. In: Stiglitz J, Yusuf S (eds) Rethinking the East Asian Miracle. World Bank and Oxford University Press, New York, pp 509–526

4. A Free Trade Agreement Policy for the Northeast Asian Countries and ASEAN: A View from People's Republic of China[1]

Angang Hu

1. Regional Free Trade Agreements as a Main Feature of Economic Globalization

Sustainable development requires an open economy, and free trade is a basic condition for an open economy. This is true for all countries and regions. Free trade has become one of the most significant trends in world development. Currently, among 206 countries and regions in the world, 107 have signed free trade agreements (FTA) with other countries and regions.

Regional free trade agreements have become a feature of international trade. The FTA of the European Union will soon expand to take in a number of countries in Central and Eastern Europe. In the Americas, FTAs already incorporate Canada, the United States, and Mexico and will soon include Chile, Brazil, and Argentina, with the eventual goal being the inclusion of 34 countries in a trade bloc by 2005. ASEAN is aiming to set up AFTA in 2003. According to an estimate by the World Trade Organization (WTO), the trading volume of FTAs made up 42% of the world's trading volume during the years 1993 to 1997 (WTO 1998). Goods traded without tariffs under the auspices of an FTA in the Americas accounted for 27% of all goods traded in the region between 1993 and 1997, up from 19% from 1988 to 1992. Mexico benefited the most. In the 1980s, the growth rate of the value of Mexico's exports of goods and services was 7%, whereas the rate rose to 14.3% in the 1990s. Meanwhile the country's GDP growth rate rose from 1.1% to 2.7% over the same period. Trade liberalization greatly increased the share of the world market accounted for by the European Union and North America. According to *The Economist* (November 9, 2000), the total value of exports originating in the European Union rose from 34.7% of the world total to 38% during the years 1993–1999 while that of the U.S. increased from 15.7% to 17.7%. At the same time, the export value of other areas of the world decreased by 5.3%.

2. FTA Between Northeast Asia and ASEAN is an Important Step Toward the Economic Development of the People's Republic of China

Why is People's Republic of China (China) focused on establishing a regional FTA with Northeast Asian countries and ASEAN?

First, the real degree of China's economic openness is relatively low. According to foreign trade calculated by exchange rate, China enjoys a highly open economy. However, if calculated in terms of purchasing power parity (PPP), the degree of openness is rather low (Fig. 1), i.e., 9.5% of GDP in 2000. The degree of openness of the United States and Japan were respectively 21.1% and 25.6% in 2000 using the same method of calculation. The import and export value of China's merchandise trade made up 3.44% and 3.92%, respectively, of the world's total in 2000, which is lower than China's population and GDP (PPP) as proportion of the world's total, with the population and GDP figures suggesting that China's import trade should have accounted for 20.8% of the world total and exports for 12.1% in 2000 (World Bank 2001: Tables 1, 4).

Second, China's long-term goal is to attain economic development through setting up an open economy. During the last two decades, China's model of trade was an export-oriented one based on the Northeast Asian model. I call this the "half-open model", with open or free trade on the export side and protectionism on the import side. China now needs to shift from an export-oriented economy to a new model of an open economy. The Chinese government has put forward an explicit plan for this goal in its Tenth Five-Year (2001–2005) Plan. The country now aims to fully open up the domestic market and promote liberalization of both trade and investment.

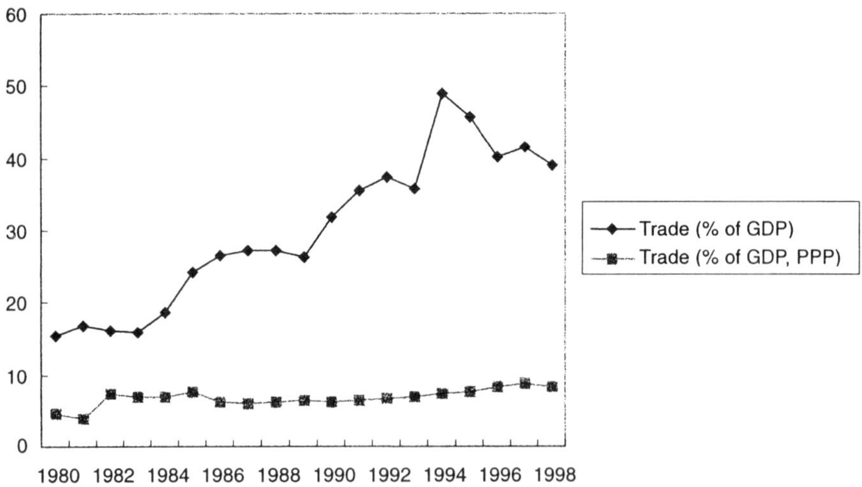

Fig. 1. China's dependence on foreign trade, 1980–1998. Source: World Bank 2000

Table 1. Key indicators of economic development for Northeast Asian countries and ASEAN (2000)

	Population millions	GDP (PPP) $ billions	Merchandise exports $ millions	Merchandise imports $ millions
Cambodia	12	17	590	700
China	1261	4965.7	249212	225097
Hong Kong, China	7	174.5	202440	214200
Indonesia	210	597.6	62016	33547
Japan	127	3354.5	479328	379514
Korea	47	820	172620	160493
Lao PDR	5	8	300	560
Malaysia	23	194.5	98237	82210
Myanmar	46		1310	2450
Philippines	76	319.2	40000	34600
Singapore	4	121	137953	134675
Thailand	61	384.6	68920	62040
Vietnam	79	159.1	14306	15200
Total	1958	11274.8	1527232	1345286
World	6054	41053	6350105	6550720
% of world's total	32.3	27.46	24.05	20.54

Source: World Bank 2001: Tables 1, 4

Note: PPP = Purchasing Power Parity

Third, China has joined the WTO as a move toward setting up an open economy. Participation in the WTO provides a good opportunity for China to take part in economic globalization, and also provides a systematic framework, or set of international game rules, for this participation. As noted in *The Economist* (November 9, 2000), it is not surprising that China has joined the WTO. It shows that developing countries are seeking to be the new winners in the global economy, and are trying to promote economic growth with new arrangements.

Fourth, the second step necessary for China to establish an open economy is the conclusion of a Free Trade Agreement (FTA) between Northeast Asia and ASEAN so as to accelerate regional economic integration. Such a step would give China a chance to learn from its partners and participate in both global and regional trade protocols.

Fifth, the Chinese government has decided to work to more fully integrate the western regions of the country into the domestic and international economy by strengthening economic and infrastructural ties running east to west across the country. This "go west" policy seeks to attract investment into the western regions of China from ASEAN nations weaving the western regions more thoroughly into the fabric of regional and international trade.

3. Northeast Asia and ASEAN Need to Become One of the Biggest FTAs in the World

According to recent theories on trade, bilateral or multilateral trade growth follows the law of "gravity". That is, bilateral or multilateral trade volumes are in direct proportion to the respective market scale of the countries involved (e.g., GDP calculated by PPP), and in inverse proportion to the distance or transaction costs involved (e.g., tariff and non-tariff barriers).

Hong Kong, Japan, and Korea (Republic of Korea) are China's largest trading and investing partners. In 1999, the total trade volume between mainland China and the three areas reached $135 billion, accounting for 37.4% of the total foreign trade volume of China. The three areas are also the main investment partners of mainland China. In 1999, foreign direct investment (FDI) from the three areas was $20.6 billion, accounting for 51.5% of the total FDI attracted to China. In addition, the three areas are the largest source for tourists to China, accounting for 88.6% of the total number of tourists visiting China.

In contrast, the volume off trade between China and ASEAN was $27.2 billion in the same year, accounting for 7.5% of China's total foreign trade volume and 4% of the total foreign trade volume of ASEAN. The volume of trade between China and Singapore was $8.56 billion, accounting for 2.4% of China's total foreign trade volume, while the volume of trade with Malaysia was $5.3 billion, or 1.5 %, of the total, and that with Indonesia was $4.8 billion, or 1.3% of the total in the same year (National Bureau of Statistics of the People's Republic of China; China 2000).

According to the World Bank's "World Development Report 2002", the total population of Northeast Asia and ASEAN accounts for one-third (32.3%) of the world's total population, and GDP (PPP) is one quarter (27.24%) of the world's total. The import and export values of East Asia's merchandise trade respectively accounted for 23% and 26% of the world's total. This compares with the United States, Canada and Mexico, which comprise the North America Free Trade Agreement (NAFTA), which accounted for 26 % of the world's imports in terms of value and 19% of the world's exports in the same year.

Northeast Asia and ASEAN together outweigh other regions in terms of population as well as enjoying the highest economic growth rate,with the exclusion of Japan, and the fastest trade-volume growth in the world. However, regional trade and investment liberalization lags behind in this part of the world and Northeast Asian and ASEAN countries have some of the world's highest market barriers. This situation seriously confines the region's potential for economic and trade growth. On the other hand, the creation of an ASEAN+3 FTA would stimulate regional economic and trade growth, and is thus likely to accelerate regional economic integration.

When an FTA encompassing Northeast Asia and ASEAN is established, it will be the one of the largest in the world. If we assume that participation in global economic integration is the basic strategy of China, accelerating the economic integration of Northeast Asia and ASEAN should be thought of as a step toward further integration with the international economy on the part of China.

Table 2. Key indicators of GDP per capita and human development index for Northeast Asia and ASEAN

	GDP per capita (PPP) $ 2000	GDP per capita $ 2000[a]	Average annual growth of GDP 1990/2000[a](%)	Life expectancy at birth 1999[a]	Under 5 mortality rate (per 1000) 1999[a]	Adult illiteracy (% of population > 15) 1999[a]	Average educational school years of (population > 15) 1999[b]	Human Development Index1999[c,d]
Cambodia	1410	260	4.6	54	143	61	—	—
China	3940	840	10.3	70	37	17	7.11	0.719 (87)
Hong Kong, China	25660	25950	4.0	80	5	7	9.41	0.880 (24)
Indonesia	2840	570	4.2	66	52	14	4.99	0.677 (102)
Japan	26460	34210	1.3	81	4	—	9.47	0.928 (9)
Korea	17340	8910	5.7	73	9	2	10.84	0.875 (27)
Lao PDR	1530	290	6.5	54	143	53	—	0.476 (130)
Malaysia	8360	3380	7.0	72	10	13	6.80	0.774 (56)
Myanmar	1027	—	—	43	203	57	—	0.551 (118)
Philippines	4220	1040	3.2	69	41	5	8.21	0.749 (70)
Singapore	30100	24740	7.8	78	4	8	7.05	0.876 (26)
Thailand	6330	2010	4.2	69	33	5	6.50	0.757 (66)
Vietnam	2030	390	7.9	69	42	7	—	0.682 (101)

[a]World Bank 2001: Tables 1–3

[b]Barro and Lee 2000:36

[c]UNDP 2001: Table 1, except data for China, which is from National Bureau of Statistics of People's Republic of China (NBSC)

[d]Data in parentheses indicate ranking among 162 countries

4. Northeast Asia and ASEAN Have Different Advantages and Disadvantages

Northeast Asia and ASEAN are at different developmental stages with distinct comparative advantages and disadvantages. This creates both competitive and cooperative relationships.

Northeast Asia and ASEAN countries are at different income levels, a situation that could almost be described as "One Asia, Four Worlds" (Table 2). In terms of GDP per capita in US dollars, Japan, Singapore, and Hong Kong are in the category of high-income countries (first world), close to the average for this category of $25,690. Taiwan, Korea, and Malaysia are in the upper-middle income group (second world), where the average income level is $8,520. Thailand, the Philippines, China, and Indonesia are in the in lower-middle income group (third world), where the average amounts to $4,170, while other ASEAN countries count among the low-income countries (fourth world), whose average income level is only is $1,870 (World Bank 2001).

Countries in Northeast Asia and ASEAN are at different human development levels, a situation that could be described as "One Asia, Three Levels". Measured by the human development index (HDI), Japan, Singapore, Hong Kong, and Korea have a high HDI (first level), at a level above 0.8 in world terms; most countries in the region have a middle HDI (second level), where HDI ranges between 0.5 and 0.799; Laos has a low HDI (third level), at a level of less than 0.5 (Table 2).

Northeast Asia and ASEAN countries have different levels of global competitiveness. The global competitiveness of an economy is defined as the capacity to achieve high rates of economic growth on a sustainable basis as reported in the "Global Competitiveness Report" compiled by the World Economic Forum and Harvard University. Global competitiveness includes two indices; the current competitiveness index, which aims to measure the conditions that determine a nation's sustainable level of productivity, and the growth competitiveness index, which measures factors that contribute to a high rate of growth in GDP per capita. In terms of the growth competitiveness index, Singapore counted second among 59 countries covered in 2000 following the United States; Hong Kong ranked eighth and Japan twenty-first. Malaysia, Korea and Thailand were ranked 29, 31, and 37, respectively, whereas China was in position 41. In terms of the current competitiveness index, all Northeast Asian and ASEAN countries showed poorer performance than in terms of the growth competitiveness index (Table 3).

Countries in Northeast Asia and ASEAN have different comparative advantages and disadvantages (Table 4). The vertical division of labor or cooperation between China and Northeast Asia is notable. The economic and trading complementarities are strong. Because they are at different development levels, labor costs in China's urban and coastal regions are very low when compared with other countries in Northeast Asia. This is an obvious comparative advantage in labor-intensive production. According to the World Bank, during the period from 1995 to 1999 the annual cost of each manufacturing laborer was $729 in China, $13,539 in Hong Kong, $31,687

Table 3. Competitiveness Ranking for Northeast Asia and ASEAN, 2000

	Growth competitiveness ranking		Current competitiveness ranking
Singapore	2	Singapore	9
Hong Kong, China	8	Japan	14
Taiwan	11	Hong Kong, China	16
Japan	21	Taiwan	21
Malaysia	25	Korea	27
Korea	29	Malaysia	30
Thailand	31	Thailand	40
Philippines	37	China	44
China	41	Philippines	46
Indonesia	44	Indonesia	47
Vietnam	53	Vietnam	53

Source: World Economic Forum and Center for International Development of Harvard University 2000

Table 4. Comparative advantages and disadvantages and international competitive power of China, Hong Kong, Korea, and Japan

	Comparative advantages	Comparative disadvantages
China	Abundant resources to provide agricultural products; Labor-intensive products; Technological products; Architectural materials and energy; Abundant labor force; Expanding human resources.	Comparative lack of capital, advanced equipment, high technology and management experience; Lack of several major resources.
Hong Kong, China	Favorable capital market and financing power; Channels to international market and management experience; Fine infrastructure and traffic conditions.	Lack of land, energy, and industrial materials; Lack of skilled labor force; Comparatively high labor costs.
Korea	Capital, relatively advanced technology and equipment; IT industry.	Lack of energy and industrial resources; Comparatively high labor costs.
Japan	Large amount of surplus capital; Advanced technology and inventions; Ability to manufacture equipment; Approved business management experience; Advanced IT industry.	Serious lack of energy and industrial resources; Overly high labor costs; Exorbitant costs for production and operation.

in Japan, and $10,743 in Korea. These figures correspond to 18.6, 43.5 and 14.7 times that of China. China and the ASEAN countries (except Singapore) are at similar development levels. Their relationship is horizontally competitive.

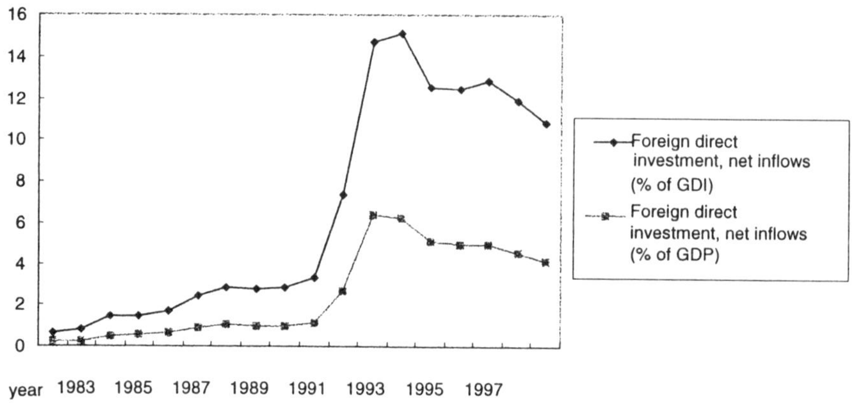

Fig. 2. China's dependence on foreign direct investment, 1982–1999. Source: World Bank 2000

Table 5. Index of Economic Freedom ranking for Northeast Asia and ASEAN, 2001

	Ranking	Overall score	Trade	Foreign direct investment
Cambodia	42	2.60	2.0	3.0
China	121	3.55	5.0	4.0
Hong Kong, China	1	1.35	1.0	1.0
Indonesia	105	3.35	3.0	3.0
Japan	35	2.45	2.0	3.0
Korea	38	2.50	3.0	3.0
Lao PDR	151	4.55	5.0	5.0
Malaysia	79	3.10	4.0	4.0
Philippines	70	2.95	3.0	3.0
Singapore	2	1.55	1.0	1.0
Thailand	32	2.40	2.0	3.0
Vietnam	137	3.85	5.0	5.0

Source: Heritage Foundation 2001

Northeast Asia and ASEAN are rated differently on indices of global economic freedom. Each country's commitment to free trade is measured by its demonstrated ability and willingness to meet objective measurable criteria such as those used in constructing the index of global economic freedom. The survey of 155 countries around the world undertaken by the Heritage Foundation and *The Wall Street Journal* in 2001 saw Hong Kong and Singapore taking the first and second spots as the world's "freest" economies, with indices of global economic freedom of between 1.00 and 1.95. Thailand, Japan, Korea, and Cambodia were found to have "free" economies with an index of global economic freedom of between 2.00 and 2.95. The Philippines, Malaysia, China, Indonesia, and Vietnam are "mostly free" economies with an index of global economic freedom of between 3.00 and 3.95 (Table 5).

In the future China will become the single largest base for labor-intensive manufacturing in the world. China is the largest of ten newly emerging markets, accounting for 40% of the total population of these ten nations, 42% of combined GDP (PPP), and one-third of trade. Labor costs are a key factor influencing a country's competitive power. In the Northeast Asian region, manufacturing labor costs are high, thus the center of the manufacturing industry is shifting to China. In fact, China is already the world's largest manufacturing base for household electric appliances, according to *Business Week of Japanese Economy* (November 27, 2000). For instance, the output of television sets in China makes up 36.2% of the world's total output, Chinese production of washing machines accounts for 23.5% of the world total, production of air-conditioners in China is 50.1% of the world total, refrigerators 21.1%, and motorcycles a particularly impressive 48.9%.

5. Influence of an FTA Between China, Japan, and Korea

The objectives for setting up an FTA between countries include the elimination of trade barriers and investment obstacles, heightening the ability to obtain resources from a broader range of sources, more effective utilization of resources, and an increase in profit in relation to resource input. In general countries benefiting most from free trade are those with the fewest trade barriers or largest trading volume, and countries with the largest profit increase from free trade are those that undertake the greatest market-opening measures. According to estimates by the World Bank and the IMF if free trade agreements covering the entire world were put in place about $250–550 billion worth of gains would be generated, of which the developing countries would account for one-third or two-fifths, depending on the source of the estimate. On the basis of a study completed by Inkyo Cheong of the International Economic Policy Research Institute, implementing free trade in Northeast Asia will markedly increase trade volumes in the region. The static gain, that is new volumes of exports, will reach $107.3 billion increasing by 15.2% on average each year. In this case, Japan will benefit the most. Its new volume of exports will be $60.6 billion, increasing annually by 15.6%. China will rank second, with new volumes of exports reaching $24 billion, increasing at 13.1% on average. Korea's new volumes of exports will be $22.7 billion, which is the single largest increase at 17.2% (Table 6). China's new volume of exports to Korea would be $4.7 billion and to Japan $19.3 billion. The new volume of exports from Korea to China would be $22.4 billion and that from Japan $52.1 billion. This indicates that Japan and Korea have a greater international competitive capacity than China. On the one hand, China will increase exports of labor-intensive agricultural products and manufactured goods to Japan and Korea. On the other hand, because of the opening of local markets, Japan and Korea will export more capital-intensive and technology-intensive products to China. This will cause China's trade surplus with Japan and Korea under trade protection (about $16.7 billion in 1997) to turn into a substantial trade deficit (estimated as $50.5 billion; Table 7).

Table 6. Customs Tariffs of China, Hong Kong, Japan, and Korea (Unit: %)

		All goods			Primary products		Manufactured goods	
		Arithmetical average	S.D.	Weighted average	Arithmetical average	Weighted average	Arithmetical average	Weighted average
China	1992	41.3	30.8	32.6	36.7	14.3	42.4	36.5
	1998	16.8	11.1	15.7	16.5	21.1	16.9	14.7
Hong Kong, China	1988	0.0	0.0	0.0	0.0	0.0	0.0	0.0
	1998	0.0	0.0	0.0	0.0	0.0	0.0	0.0
Japan	1988	5.9	8.0	3.3	10.4	3.7	4.7	2.9
	1999	4.8	7.3	2.3	8.6	4.0	3.4	1.4
Korea	1988	18.8	8.1	13.8	19.8	8.1	18.7	16.9
	1999	8.7	5.9	5.9	12.8	5.5	7.8	6.1

Source: World Bank 2001, Table 6.6

Note: SD = Standard Deviation

Table 7. Influence of tariff elimination on increase of exports from China, Korea, and Japan (Unit: $ millions)

Source/Destiny	Korea	Japan	China	Total
Korea		332.00	22385.67	22717.67
Japan	8506.73		52122.21	60628.94
China	4664.93	19310.44		23975.37
Total increase				107321.98

Source: Inkyo 1999

Table 8. Influence of tariff elimination on the trade balances of China, Korea, and Japan (Unit: $ millions)

	Korea	Japan	China	Expected regional trade balance[a]	Trade balance (1997)
Korea		-8173.73	17720.74	9546.01	-9680
Japan	8174.73		32811.77	40986.47	-6999
China	-17720.74	-32811.77		-50532.51	16679

[a]Refers to trade between China, Japan and Korea

Source: Inkyo 1999

We must have an objective understanding of this issue. First, the international competitiveness of China is obviously less than that of Japan or Korea (Table 3). This is the major factor behind what would be trade deficits for China. Due to the large increase in import volumes, competition in home markets would be also intensified, which can be beneficial in enhancing the competitiveness of domestic enterprises. Secondly, an FTA can be carried out in stages giving domestic enterprises time to adjust and accommodate themselves to the new circumstances. Third, China has the ability to assimilate the cost of such changes. During the Ninth Five-Year Plan (1996–2000) China's trade surplus was $149.5 billion, averaging about $30 billion per year. This means the country can assimilate the cost of changes to the way in which trade is conducted within five years. Fourth, though China would have a trade deficit with Japan and Korea, it would still have a rather large trade surplus with other countries, which would compensate for the deficit. Fifth, as a middle or lower income country, China need not adopt a trade surplus strategy with regard to more advanced countries. On the contrary, with a view to ensuring a sound balance of international trade (e.g., controlled at under 3%–5%), it should open up its markets, and import more high technology capital goods (while limiting imports of consumer goods), so as to facilitate the acquisition of technological resources from the outside world. Sixth, after establishing an FTA, FDI from Japan and Korea will markedly increase which will compensate for the imbalance of international income and expenses to a large extent by increasing net income. The inflow of net capital would play an important role in compensating for any negative impact elsewhere.

6. Objectives and Design of an FTA

The establishment of an FTA will advance the free trade agenda. An FTA incorporating China should be founded on a genuine commitment to open markets. A country's openness is related to its trade policy, capital flow and foreign investment, property rights, and level of regulation. Under a liberal trade regime there is broad freedom to trade; freedom to invest; freedom to operate a business without excessive tax or regulatory burdens; and security of investment (Hulsman et al. 2001). These guidelines should be applied in laying out any FTA plan for Northeast Asia and other countries in the region as they represent a sensible route to free trade for both the global economy and Northeast Asia.

For long-term development, the following objectives of an FTA can be carried out simultaneously or step by step:

1. Establishment of an FTA between China, Japan, Korea, and Hong Kong.
2. Establishment of an FTA between China and ASEAN.
3. Establishment of a Northeast Asia FTA incorporating the above two FTA's.
4. Incorporation of South Asian countries in the above FTA frameworks.
5. Establishment of a framework for free trade across the Asia-Pacific region.

An FTA covering Northeast Asia and the ASEAN countries would be based on the framework of the WTO and aimed at establishing a fair, stable, free trade environment including liberalization of goods and services trading, investment and capital, and also including international cooperation in the areas of the economy, technology, education and culture.

To realize these goals, it is necessary to adhere to the tenets of the WTO, and to handle bilateral or multilateral trade disputes according to WTO regulations. It is also necessary to take a flexible approach. In some sensitive areas (such as agriculture), it might be acceptable to carry out trade liberalization gradually. Moreover, it is crucial to establish a multilateral strategic trading relationship, rather than promote only regional trade liberalization, ensuring that any partners in a regional FTA also participate in larger efforts to promote global trade liberalization.

To create an FTA that meets these goals it is necessary to reduce import tariffs and calculate real tariffs. It is also necessary for all the partners in an FTA to set tariffs consistent for all sides. A schedule for reducing and canceling tariffs must be put in place with the goal of realizing meaningful free trade within 5–10 years. It is important that all parties to such an agreement avoid putting new trade barriers in place. Issues concerning the origin of goods can be classified according to the rules of the WTO, which apply added-value as a standard for calculating tariffs.

It is also essential that various non-tariff trade barriers be eliminated, and import permits be reduced. Paperless trading and e-commerce should be encouraged and customs procedures simplified. Customs cooperation should heightened to establish a uniform process based on the international customs clearance protocol. Governments should be encouraged to adopt e-purchasing and public bidding techniques in purchasing and public investment projects. Standardized customs clearance procedures, goods supply and after-service systems, and information- and data-sharing systems must also be established. It is also important to investigate and prosecute cases of bribery and corruption in a cooperative manner.

Active promotion of trade liberalization in the service industry sector is also a key component of any FTA process. At present, one-fifth of the world's trade is connected with the service industry. Northeast Asia and ASEAN are areas with a low service trading rate and a high market potential. In terms of future development, when service trade may exceed the growth of the manufacturing business, the service industry itself will create demand for the manufacturing sector. The proportion of workers employed in the service industry in China is less than one-third, whereas that of other industries is above 60%. An open service market is key to promoting development of the service industry and increasing employment opportunities. With the exception of government services and a few special services, it is necessary to fully open the service market. The government should not hold shares, directly interfere, or manage social services. This means that the government should invest or fund, but not directly engage in production, management or daily operations in this sector. Meanwhile, the government should encourage competition between public institutions and private enterprises, foreign companies, and domestic organizations. Governmental interference in the service industry should be discouraged, and complicated regulations simplified. Potential investors should be judged without discrimination. Regulations must be transparent, stable and fair.

It is also essential that WTO regulations and other international protocols on intellectual property rights be respected. This is a significant condition for establishing a knowledge-based economy, and is also important in the quest to obtain outside knowledge and strengthen economic competitiveness. Protecting intellectual property rights would benefit not only other countries, but would also encourage innovation within China, stimulating creativity and commercial application of new ideas.

A successful approach to free trade and economic liberalization also encourages competition. Monopoly or anti-competition policies not only distort the economic environment, but also create serious barriers to the liberalization of trade and investment. In contrast, competition-encouraging policies are helpful in effectively exerting natural market pressures to ensure the effective allocation of resources. This means governments would be well advised to promote free and fair competition and reduce and reverse distortions and monopolization in trade and investment, emphasizing broad cooperation based on fair competition.

7. Priority Fields for FTA Cooperation in the Near Future

7.1 Human Resources Development and International Cooperation in Science and Technology

Governments should aim to provide financial aid to encourage knowledge sectors of the economy, such as universities and research institutes, to cooperate in human resources development and set up regional networks of education, scientific research, information, and environmental monitoring, so as to provide knowledge infrastructure investment and human resources to establish a knowledge-based economy. Governments should also encourage scientists, professors and technicians to give lectures, pursue exchange studies, and take short-term positions in institutions in countries with which ties are being forged.

7.2 Funding and Increasing Chances for Exchange Students and Professionals

Governments should work to strengthen exchange in the cultural and other fields. Efforts should also be made to encourage non-governmental academic exchange, information exchange (e.g., public databases), and intellectual property rights exchange (e.g., patent license, training courses for trademark protection, international exhibition of technical products, and software copyright transferring). Patent application procedures should be simplified and an Asia-wide patent system established if feasible. It is also important to provide platforms for training and exchange, such as remote education networks, remote medical networks, and remote conference networks. Technological and professional exchanges between small- and medium-sized enterprises should be encouraged. In significant scientific research fields, e.g., information technology, biotechnology, medicine, new materials, new energy and resources, and environment protection technology, international cooperation should be promoted through such means as setting up international laboratories, and encouraging publication of co-authored academic papers.

7.3 International Cooperation of Energy and Environment Protection

The energy consumption of Northeast Asia accounts for 19.3% of the world total. The emission of CO_2 is 21.9%, with China responsible for two-thirds of this. Therefore, it is necessary to establish energy-saving and environmental protection policies. Through trading in CO_2 emissions, it is possible to economically reduce the CO_2 emission of this area (especially China). Meanwhile, the active promotion of cooperation in the areas of energy and environmental protection, and commercialization of technology in these areas, should be promoted.

7.4 Open Up Market of Information and Service Industries

The information technology industry in China is now enjoying explosive growth in a so-called leapfrog pattern. China should open up its IT product manufacturing industry to Northeast Asia and ASEAN, and actively develop production bases and material flow delivery of international IT products, such as telecommunications and household IT products and services, cable, Internet services and e-commerce businesses. The actively promotion of international cooperation in telecommunications services should be made a priority with a sharp reduction in international telecommunications fees. Competition should be discouraged and training for IT professionals made available, while e-business and paperless trading develops apace. The establishment of privacy protection and authentication systems is of great importance. The Chinese market, in particular, should be opened up to allow outside firms to win construction of information and telecommunications infrastructure contracts.

7.5 Opening the Tourism Market and Improving Cooperation Across the Industry Throughout the Trading Area

China has designated tourism as a future priority industry. According to the statistics of the World Tourism Organization, tourism income presently makes up more than 10% of the world's total income, while in terms of employment it accounts for over 12% of the world total. In 1999, the tourism income of China was less than 5% of GDP, and the industry employed less than 2% of the population. In the same year, the number of tourists from Hong Kong, Japan and Korea entering China came to 64.52 million, accounting for 88.6% of the total number of tourists entering China. These countries and regions provide the greatest proportion of visitors to China. Opening up the tourism market will accelerate the development of tourism, and speed regulation of the tourism market. China should open the tourism market first to northeast Asia and ASEAN, so as to drive related industries to open and develop. For example, opening up the tourism market will encourage development of civil aviation and air express delivery services and promote cooperative production involving small- and medium-sized airlines. This approach would also help to develop the tourist resources of small- and medium-sized cities, especially in central and western China. Such an approach would also promote the development of aviation across borders, encouraging cooperation in areas such as air rescue, air exploration, tourism by air and other fields.

7.6 Active Organization of an Asian Monetary Fund, with Effective Mechanisms to Deal with Financial Crises and Promote Financial Reform

China, Japan, Korea, and Hong Kong have the largest foreign exchange reserves in the world, but they lack a system for preventing financial risk. Therefore, it is crucial to establish an Asian Monetary Fund in cooperation with the IMF, the World Bank, and the Asian Development Bank. This effort would be aimed at preventing and monitoring financial risk, promoting regional cooperation, and establishing a regional stock market. In 1999, the market value of the stocks listed in the three countries and one region was $3,480 billion, accounting for 12.7% of the world's total, far less than that of North America, particularly in relation to the United States, which accounts for about 51.5% of the world total. With the exception of Japan, stock markets in the other three areas are too small, putting them under the direct influence of the American market. To reduce the risks of fluctuation, it is necessary to establish a regional stock market, and encouraging individual and institutional investors in all the partner states to invest in firms based in partner states. Once a regional stock market if formed, it is possible to gradually expand its influence, eventually absorbing bourses in Singapore and Malaysia.

References

Barro RJ, Lee J-W (2000) International data on educational attainment: updates and implications. CID Working Paper 42 (April)

Cheong I (1999) Economic integration in Northeast Asia: searching for a feasible approach. KIEP Working Paper 99-25. Korea Institute for International Economic Policy, Seoul

China (2000) China Statistical Yearbook 2000. China Statistics Press, Beijing

Heritage Foundation (2001) [www.heritage.org/views/2001/ed041901.html]

Hulsman JC, O'Driscoll GP Jr, Froning DH (2001) The Free Trade Association: A trade agenda for the new global economy [www.heritage.org]

UNDP (2001) Human development report 2001: human development indicators. Oxford University Press, New York

World Bank (2001) World development report 2002: building institutions for markets. Oxford University Press, New York

World Economic Forum and Center for International Development of Harvard University (2000) The competitiveness report 2000. Oxford University Press, New York

WTO (1998) Preferential and non-preferential trade flows in the world. World Trade Organization staff paper (September)

Notes

[1] This paper was prepared for the Chinese government on 12 February 2001; a second draft was presented at an international conference in the Republic of Korea (Korea) on 27-28 November 2001.

5. Asia's Future: Strategic Economic Cooperation or Balkanization?

Walden Bello

1. Introduction

Let me begin by noting that there was a quality of desperation in Prime Minister Koizumi's swing through the ASEAN countries in January 2002. A Vietnamese official I was speaking with at the time told me that it seemed to be a hastily put-together affair that was all show and little substance whose main purpose was not stated, and that served to counter the proposal floated by People's Republic of China (China) in October 2001 to form a free trade zone with ASEAN.

The proposal for accelerated strategic economic cooperation is one that should have been floated at least a decade ago, when Japan, Korea (Republic of Korea), and ASEAN were enjoying a considerable degree of growth and prosperity. Now the Japanese economy and the ASEAN economies are in deep crisis, providing a very difficult context for negotiating closer economic relationships.

A decade has been wasted that could have been devoted to arriving at some form of economic arrangement that would have carried forward and transformed the informal integration that already began in the 1980s. Why was the momentum lost?

2. Fear of Washington

In my view, the fault lies on both sides. In the case of Japan, it was fear of Washington. The early 1990s were the time when APEC was being pushed by the United States and Australia as a trans-Pacific free trade area. Japan did not want to antagonize Washington, so it did not endorse any opposing mode of regional integration. It wanted especially to distance itself from anything that might be seen as supporting the proposal for an East Asia Economic Grouping, a vision of a unified economic bloc involving ASEAN, China, the Koreas, and Japan, proposed by Prime Minister Mahathir of Malaysia.

Far more serious in its consequences was Japan's failure to carry through with its proposal for the creation of an Asian Monetary Fund (AMF), which would have pooled the reserves of the more prosperous countries and to which members whose currencies were under speculative attack would have access.

I think that the damage done to the credibility of Japan by its backing down on this issue was very great. Many Asian governments thought that with the establishment of the Fund, the outcome could have been very different. Instead they were left to the mercy of the International Monetary Fund (IMF) and Washington, split in their strategies for survival, with only Malaysia brave enough to follow a path that defied the IMF. It is true that funds were later allocated to the region under the Miyazawa Plan, but this was only within the framework of IMF stabilization programs and only after the major ASEAN economies had collapsed.

It was a terrible diplomatic debacle for Japan, one that reinforced the perception of many Asians that Tokyo had not shaken off the psychology of the Occupation when it came to dealing with Washington.

3. ASEAN: Loss of Direction

The ASEAN governments were not without fault in the proccss, however. They supported the AMF for obvious reasons, but except for Mahathir, there were no leaders or governments who were really serious about moving on to higher levels of integration and more fully coordinated economic policies. One can say that they were satisfied with the level and the mode of informal integration that had been achieved already in manufacturing. They saw no good reason to move further or to formalize economic institutions to govern at the level of integration already achieved.

Perhaps the hesitation sprang from the fact that the ASEAN governments were themselves having problems carrying through their integration at the ASEAN level. It is true that in the early 1990s, the ASEAN Free Trade Area (AFTA) had been negotiated, but this was initially above all a defensive move in response to the threat of an APEC free trade area. However, the pace of actual trade liberalization remained slow throughout the 1990s. Indeed, it was hardly proceeding at all, owing partly to the desire of different governments to protect their prized agricultural commodities and their industrial elites.

As to industrial integration, programs such as the ASEAN Industrial Complementation Scheme had either withered on the vine or been utilized mainly by Japanese corporations to rationalize the distribution of industrial plants they were in the process of relocating from Japan to Southeast Asia. Industrial integration was in progress, but it was one following the logic of subsidization of Toyota, Nissan, Matsushita, and Fujitsu, one that was directed at creating a manufacturing base from which to assault the American market without being subjected to sanctions from the United States.[1] This was hardly the type of integration that the founders of ASEAN had in mind, but it was one that their successors allowed to transpire owing to their own lack of capacity to pursue a different project.

The failure of a more directed industrial integration contrasted with the late 1960s. ASEAN was unsure of where to bring trade and industrial cooperation in the 1990s. I think it is fair to say that there were two simultaneous directions and that the tension between the two was never really resolved.

One direction was toward the reduction of trade barriers among the ASEAN countries as a prelude to their participation in a broader free trade area like APEC, in a word, a step toward global free trade. One might say that the technocrats in Singapore and Manila thought in this fashion.

The other direction was advocated by those who saw the lowering of mutual tariffs as a move toward a different strategic objective, i.e., the creation of a large, protected regional market that would serve as a base for regional import substitution. This use of trade policy for purposes of industrialization, which many technocrats in Indonesia and Malaysia shared, was, in fact, the original thrust of the United Nations-sponsored "Robinson Report" that had served as the intellectual and policy inspiration for ASEAN in the early 1960s (see Bello and Chavez-Malaluan 1996).

For all intents and purposes, ASEAN remained primarily a political project, and in contrast to the lagging AFTA, the expansion of the ASEAN Regional Forum (ARF) absorbed the energies of ASEAN governments in the mid- to late 1990s, when the ambition of ASEAN to play effective balance-of-power politics vis-à-vis China, Japan, and the United states was decisively disrupted by the Asian financial crisis.

4. Fatal Flaw

Perhaps a fatal problem in ASEAN, one that would also dog other projects such as the Asian Monetary Fund, the East Asia Economic Grouping, and the ASEAN+3 currency arrangement (including ASEAN countries and Japan, Korea, and China), is that it remained an elite project. The nature, purpose, and direction of these groupings were discussed mainly among technocratic and political elites. The people were never brought into the equation in terms of mobilizing them to support these arrangements.

The ASEAN project, for instance, was never democratized, and this failure did not stem from the so-called authoritarian–democratic divide among the ASEAN governments. Neither the Philippine government under Corazon Aquino nor the Indonesian government under Suharto was really interested in involving their citizens actively in the ASEAN enterprise. Not surprisingly, "ASEAN brotherhood" remains a laughable idea, except perhaps among chief executives and diplomats. In fact, although it was established much later than ASEAN, Mercosur in Latin America enjoys a greater resonance in the popular consciousness of the citizenries of the participating governments than ASEAN among the peoples of Southeast Asia.

The problem in not bringing people actively in is that once the will at the top falters, there is no momentum below to keep things moving. The opposite of this is illustrated in the European Union: if you move too fast at the top and do not bring people along, they will slow you down at some point, as the Danes and other citizenries did in the European Union in response to the Maastricht Treaty.

5. Strategic Cooperation and Survival

My intention in highlighting the problems in achieving more coordinated economic policy-making and integration in the sphere of economics is not to throw cold water on this project. It is simply to underline how much political will is necessary to push through an utterly necessary enterprise. I think there is widespread realization in government, economic, and academic circles by now that without closer regional ties, most East Asian countries will be marginalized in a twenty-first-century global economy dominated by big blocs such as the European Union and the North American Free Trade Area. Some say that only China and India have the requisite combination of people, capital, skills, resources, and political strength to attain the status of effective players.

Our vulnerability as governments acting separately with a largely national-economy perspective has been brought home by the Asian financial crisis and the current global recession. In both instances, a coordinated regional response could have prevented disaster – an Asian Monetary Fund in the case of the financial crisis and a reflationary strategy pursued by a regional economic grouping in the case of the current global recession.

The need for closer strategic economic coordination and integration is not simply a response to the volatile character of the global economy but to the intensely competitive superpower economic approach that has been unleashed by the United States, especially since the end of the Cold War. Cooperation and competition have marked the economic relationship between East Asia and the United States since the end of the Second World War, but, whereas one can say that prior to the end of the Cold War, cooperation predominated owing to the priority of the anti-Communist alliance, since the early 1990s, competition if not antagonism had become the dominant feature of the relationship. Keeping Asia weak politically, economically, and militarily in the course of the 1990s was the key strategic thrust of United States policy in the region. Indeed, as Chalmers Johnson has noted, there is much to be said for the view that the IMF policies imposed on Asia in the wake of the Asian financial crisis reflected the fact that "having defeated the fascists and the communists, the United States now sought to defeat its last remaining rivals for global dominance: the nations of East Asia that had used the conditions of the Cold War to enrich themselves" (Johnson 2000: 206).

6. Necessary Conditions for Success

What are some of the necessary conditions for a successful move toward a regional economic bloc? Let me cite four, some of which have already been touched upon indirectly above.

First of all, Japan has to shake off the deep dependency it has on Washington and move toward decisively representing regional interests. This is the critical decade, when Japan has to choose between Asia and Washington. Sticking to the old policy of subservience toward Washington's dictates will guarantee slow-motion marginalization as an economic power.

Second, the leaders of ASEAN will have to jettison the crippling paradigm of free trade and free capital flows with which Washington and the IMF have straitjacketed their economies following the Asian financial crisis. They have to reorient ASEAN along the lines of the original vision of a planned, protected regional market, marked by technology sharing and a healthy, rational division of labor. This is also the perspective they should bring to the larger project of East Asian economic coordination and integration.

Third, to be sustainable, regional integration must be popularized and democratized. This means, among other things, that it must be made meaningful in terms of its benefits to the people. No longer can it be justified simply in terms of economic growth. It must be shown to have benefits in terms of ending poverty and reducing inequality both within countries and across countries. Environmental consciousness is now on the rise throughout the region, and to really catch on, regional integration must be shown to have benefits in terms of enhancing the quality of life and the quality of the environment throughout the region. This means, among other things, that Japan must stop treating Southeast Asia and China as the dumping ground for its dirty industries under the guise of regional industrial integration.

Mobilizing people in support of a project of regional integration will necessitate not just promises from above but making sure that institutions created include those allowing participation by labor unions, peasant organizations, environmental organizations, and other civil organizations in the decision-making process. The days when technocrats, politicians, and industrial elites monopolized decision making when it came to regional coordination are over. Whatever one thinks about civil groups or NGOs, they are on the rise and they will make tremendous demands for inclusion in decision-making in this decade. We have to learn from the experience of the European post-Maastricht era that regional integration carried out with only marginal participation from electorates and society at large ultimately backfires.

Finally, any Asian economic bloc that emerges must include not only ASEAN, Korea and Japan. It must most definitely include China. A regional enterprise that excludes China would eliminate one of the key sources of economic dynamism in the region. Being one of the centers of sustained growth, China's role in reflating the regional economy in what is threatening to be a decade of global deflation and recession cannot be understated. Of course, there are major problems that have to do with comparative labor costs, investment competition, and export competition that need to be sorted out, but these must be the subject of negotiations within a broader framework of strategic cooperation.

Keeping China out of any regional arrangement on the grounds that it is too big will simply play into the hands of Washington's strategy of playing off the countries in the region against one another in order to keep Asia divided and weak.

In summary, let me say that East Asia has no choice but to move toward a greater degree of strategic economic cooperation and integration. The next two decades are going to be critical. By 2020, we will either be collectively a major player in the global economy or most of us will be marginal actors in an economically Balkanized area of the world.

References

Bello W, Chavez-Malaluan J (1996) APEC versus ASEAN. In: Bello W, Chavez-Malaluan J (eds) Four adjectives in search of a noun. People's Forum on APEC, Manila

Johnson C (2000) Blowback: the costs and consequences of American empires. Holt, New York

New strategies toward super-ASEAN bloc (1992) This is [Tokyo] (August). In: FBIS Environment Report (October)

Notes

[1] The logic was described by one Japanese diplomat, Hisahiko Okazaki, as follows: "Japan is creating an exclusive Japanese market in which Asia-Pacific nations are incorporated in the so-called *keiretsu* system." The essential relationship between Japan and Southeast Asia, he contended, was one of trading "captive imports, such as products from plants in which the Japanese have invested," in return for "captive exports, such as necessary equipment and materials." [New Strategies 1992: 18].

6. Economic Development and Regional Cooperation by People's Republic of China in East Asia

Linfei Song

1. Introduction

Regional economic integration is an important way to meld into the world economy and it is a necessary period of economic development. East Asia is the region with world's largest population and fastest economic growth but regional economic cooperation has been very weak. Contradictions have not been properly solved in the region because of a mixture of external and internal forces, some historical and some continuing. Up to now there have been obstacles and a latent crisis on the road to development of regional economic cooperation in East Asia. Thus, the governments of East Asian countries and ordinary individuals need to actively adopt a more positive attitude to regional cooperation and create better conditions to ensure the realization and smooth development of regional economic cooperation.

This chapter addresses the obstacles to and the crisis in East Asian regional economic cooperation by way of seven questions and discussion.

2. What Is the Basic Framework?

What framework should be adopted in East Asian regional economic cooperation? The political leaders of the East Asian nations have made the following choices.

2.1 The Association of Southeast Asian Nations (ASEAN)

Since its foundation in August 1967, ASEAN has always been conceived as a system of multilateral security cooperation. In 1971, five Southeast Asian nations signed the Declaration of ASEAN Peace, Freedom, and Neutrality. In January 1992, the fourth ASEAN summit meeting decided to enhance the dialogue on politics and security with nations outside the region in order to realize the aims of ASEAN peace, freedom, neutrality, and a nuclear-free zone.

2.2 ASEAN Regional Forum (ARF)

Since its foundation in July 1994, this forum has played an important part in the peace of the ASEAN region. The second session, held in 1995, divided the ARF aim into three sub-aims: to strengthen trust step-by-step among Asia-Pacific nations through dialogue and consultation; to advance and further develop preventive diplomacy; and to establish an institution for security cooperation to deal with regional conflict so as to maintain and ensure the peace, stability, and prosperity of the Asia-Pacific region. At present ARF is continuing dialogue and consultation. There is still a long way to go to establishing the preventive institution and a structure of multilateral security cooperation.

2.3 ASEAN+10

ASEAN+10 is a conference between ASEAN and its ten dialogue partners, consisting of Australia, Canada, China (People's Republic of China), the European Union, India, Japan, New Zealand, Russia, Korea (Republic of Korea), and the United States.

2.4 ASEAN+1

ASEAN+1 is conference between ASEAN and a single nation with which the group is engaged.

The above four frameworks of regional cooperation are all forms of political cooperation seeking to solve the problem of national security.

The Asian financial crisis sped up the pace of East Asian regional economic cooperation. In July 1997, the crisis broke out in Thailand and spread rapidly to ASEAN and the East Asian region. This "infectious effect" not only exposed the economic defects and fragility that East Asian nations have in common, but it also reflected the economic connection and interdependency among East Asian nations. After the crisis East Asian nations came to realize that only by strengthening regional economic cooperation can a single nation increase its capability to avert the risks associated with economic globalization and retain a capacity for economic development.

2.5 ASEAN+3

ASEAN+3 is an informal meeting between the leaders of ASEAN and the China, Japan, and Korea. At an informal meeting in December 1997 in Kuala Lumpur, the leaders present sent a definite signal on the enhancement of East Asian regional political and economic cooperation. At the second ASEAN+3 conference, held in December 1998, Jingtao Hu, Vice Chairman of China, suggested holding East Asian meetings for vice finance ministers and vice governors of central banks in order to study international financial reform and to supervise and control short-term capital flows. All leaders present agreed with China's suggestion, which meant that for the first time East Asia possessed a framework for dialogue and consultation among high-level officials in important economic departments. In November 1999, the third East Asian leaders' conference was held. The main topic was how to promote East Asian regional cooperation and a Joint East Asian Statement was issued for the first time.

The fourth conference was held on November 24, 2000, in Singapore. This conference examined the specific measures needed to foster cooperation based on the Joint East Asian Statement. ASEAN+3 should become the basic framework for further East Asian regional cooperation.

3. Where to Start?

Recently East Asian nations have actively and effectively explored various modes of regional economic cooperation. These mainly include the following three programs.

3.1 Asian Currency Cooperation

The first mode for East Asian regional financial cooperation is a currency exchange system. In May 2000, the finance ministers of ASEAN and Japan, Korea, and China held a conference in Chiang Mai, Thailand. The conference decided to establish a bilateral currency exchange system under the framework of ASEAN+3 and to establish a network of contact persons to facilitate regional surveillance in East Asia, based on the Manila Framework Talks in November1997 so as to increase East Asian resilience against financial crisis. In 2000 Japan and Malaysia signed an agreement on a bilateral exchange adjustment of $1 billion; Japan also signed bilateral agreements with Thailand and Korea. The ASEAN+3 conference formally agreed to the "Asian Currency Cooperation Plan." The plan seeks first to establish a currency exchange agreement enabling exchange of financial information, and establish a supervising institution that can prevent currency crises by strengthening mutual coordination of partner nations central banks. This will enable necessary support to be obtained should the currency of one partner nation come under attack.

The present exchange agreement implies, in fact, that Japan works as the supplier of currency in international exchange. Japan and Korea can mutually exchange $7 billion in dollar–Korean won; Japan and Thailand signed a U.S. dollar-baht exchange agreement worth $3 billion; Japan and the Philippines reached an agreement worth $3 billion; Japan and Malaysia reached agreement to exchange $3.5 billion; Japan and China are discussing the establishment of a currency exchange between the yen and the yuan.

The second mode for East Asian regional financial cooperation is the establishment of an Asian Monetary Fund (AMF), as proposed by Japan. The basic function of the fund would be to establish institutional emergency financing, to prevent crisis, to change the current system for setting exchange rates, and to stabilize exchange rates. In March 2001, the finance ministers of ten nations (seven from ASEAN and three from Japan, Korea, and China) issued a statement in Brunei. It launched a plan to share foreign exchange reserves in the mode of a currency agreement, for fear of another attack on an Asian currency or currencies, until a larger "Asian Reserve Fund" is established. This conference represents a big leap forward towards the establishment of an "Asian Monetary Fund Organization."

The third mode, which has been proposed by some officials from the Philippines and Hong Kong, is the establishment of a unitary Asian currency, an "Asian dollar." This can only be a long-term aim as it can be realized only after regional free trade and investment has been firmly established and only after current and historical obstacles have been overcome.

3.2 Internationalization of the Japanese Yen

The internationalization of the yen is yet another possible means of establishing an Asian unitary currency. Is this choice feasible? For a long time Japan has been working on the establishment of a yen circle in East Asia so as to be able to play a leading role in finance. In October 1998, Japanese Finance Minister Kiichi Miyazawa suggested that Japan set up a finance aid plan of $30 billion, of which $15 billion was to be used for long-term finance aid, and $15 billion for short-term capital requirements in the region. Miyazawa pointed out that the excessive dependency on the U.S. dollar was one of the main causes of the Asian currency crisis. Therefore many countries in the region expected the yen to play a larger role. He argued that increasing use of the yen, next to the dollar and the euro, would help to stabilize the international currency system. This plan is called the "New Miyazawa Initiative." Its intention is to enlarge the use and influence of the yen in the region.

The Japanese Finance Ministry has an advisory body called the Council on Foreign Exchange and Other Transactions. In April 1999, it published a report entitled "Internationalization of the Yen in the Twenty-first Century." This report suggests measures to promote the Japanese yen as an international currency.

The plurality of Asian currencies increases exchange costs. When exporting commodities, Asian nations must sell their own currency at a low price to buy dollars or euros in order to conduct business. Japan hopes to use the yen extensively as a safety net for fear of fluctuation in the dollar or the euro. The yen is the most internationalized currency in Asia, but it does not account for a high proportion of total Asian transactions compared to the dollar and the euro. At present, 60% of the international foreign exchange transactions carried out in the region are conducted in dollars and 23% in euros. In 1999, the yen was used for only 5.1% of the transactions conducted among all nations in the region. Also, the use of the yen as an international currency is declining. From 1999 to 2000, the share of the yen value of world commodity exchanges fell by 1.4%; the rate of using yen in transactions and its share in foreign exchange reserves are both declining (Table 1). There would thus appear to be serious obstacles to the yen becoming the main currency used by other countries in international transactions. The yen should play a further role suiting

Table 1. Rate of yen value in trade exchange, capital exchange and foreign exchange reserves, 1990–2000

Year		1990	1993	1995	1997	1998	1999	2000
Bank foreign net assets								
	Yen	10.2	—	11.0	9.9	10.1	9.0	8.7
	Dollar	41.5	—	37.0	40.6	39.1	39.5	41.3
	Euro	—	—	—	—	—	27.7	26.9
Net volume of ICOI								
	Yen	—	14.0	17.3	13.7	11.7	10.5	8.6
	Dollar	—	38.9	34.3	43.8	45.3	47.1	48.7
	Euro	—	—	—	—	—	28.8	30.0
Governments' F/X reserve								
	Yen	8.0	—	6.8	5.3	5.3	5.1	—
	Dollar	50.6	—	56.8	62.1	65.7	66.2	—
	Euro	—	—	—	—	—	12.5	—

Source: Chen 2001

Notes: ICOI = International Certificate of Indebtedness; F/X = foreign exchange

Japan's economic position. Similarly, the Chinese yuan should also play a role in accordance with China's economic position. Yuan internationalization versus yen internationalization is an "ideologically" wrong viewpoint. On the contrary, it is better to seek different modes of cooperation to internationalize the yen and the yuan.

3.3 East Asian Free Trade Area

The signing of regional free trade agreements has become a basic step for all nations aiming to deepen economic trade relations. At present among all the world's main trading powers, only Korea, Japan, and China have not become members of a regional economic arrangement. From the viewpoint of the degree of dependency in trade and investment and mutual development of the industrial structure, East Asia has already met the basic requirements to develop free trade. There are three means by which ASEAN+3 can become the basic framework for East Asian economic cooperation:

3.3.1 1+1

This cooperative framework is already in place. Japan and Singapore took the first steps. From January 9–14, 2002, Japanese Prime Minister Junichiro Koizumi visited five ASEAN nations and signed his country's first free trade agreement with Singapore. The key point in the agreement is the way in which Japan opens its domestic market to Singapore. As a result of the negotiations Japan has agreed to do away with the import tariff on 3800 Singaporean goods, i.e., tariffs on 94% of commodities by value imported into Japan from Singapore. Singapore only needs to abolish tariffs on four kinds of medicinal liquor. The Japanese government hopes that this agreement will set an example for the development of Japan–East Asian relations (*Global Daily*, January 17, 2002).

The development of a Japan–Korea free trade area is also in progress. In May 2000, the Korea Institute for International Economic Policy issued a report stating that the average rate of Korean tariffs is 7.9%, against 2.9% in Japan. If Japan and Korea cancelled tariffs at the same time, the deficit in Korean trade with Japan would rapidly increase. In September 2000, a Japan–Korea summit meeting determined to seize the opportunity to advance the prospects for a Japan–Korea free trade area. If everything goes smoothly, the two governments will probably reach agreement before 2005. The construction of a Japan–Korea free trade area would help to enhance economic relations between the partners but will probably have a negative influence on Sino-Japan and Sino-Korean economic relations.

3.3.2 ASEAN+1

This mode of cooperation is also making progress. The Chinese government has adopted a proactive attitude towards East Asian regional economic cooperation. In November 2001, the Chinese government put forward in an ASEAN+3 conference the suggestion that a Sino-ASEAN free trade agreement be signed within ten years. It got a positive ASEAN response. According to an ASEAN prediction, by 2010 the total trade of the Sino-ASEAN free trade area will rise rapidly from the current $1,300 billion to almost the same level as in the European and North American free trade areas. The regional trade proportion of all the members will increase from the present 20% to 30%. The foreign capital proportion in the area will obviously witness an increase.

3.3.3 ASEAN+3

This mode of cooperation is still only theoretical. During the ASEAN+3 conference in 1999, at a meeting with Japan, Korea, and China, then Korean President Dae Jung Kim proposed for the first time establishing discussions exploring the possibility of economic cooperation among the three countries and ASEAN. The leaders reached consensus on this. During the 2000 ASEAN+3 conference, the leaders again confirmed this suggestion. Korean research shows that if both Korea and Japan were to do away with tariff barriers, the Korean deficit against Japan would increase by $7.1 billion. If China enters into the free trade area, the additional trade deficit between Korea and Japan will be compensated by the trade surplus obtained from Korea-China trade resulting in a net increase in the trade surplus of $9.5 billion. The Japanese trade surplus will increase by $41 billion. The addition, the Japanese and Korean trade surpluses, would be equivalent to the increase in China's trade deficit. If a Chinese study were to arrive at the same conclusion, China's response plan may take one of the following two forms: either a delay in the timetable for signing an agreement on a free trade area embracing Japan, Korea, and China; or asking Japan and Korea to provide compensation by investing in China. The ASEAN+3 mode of cooperation also suits frontier trade between Russia, North Korea (Democratic People's Republic of Korea), and China as well as the exploration of the Tumen drainage area. In fact, it pays if Japan and Korea take part in this approach.

3.4 Economic Technology and Development Cooperation

At present, East Asian nations have reached agreement to proceed with the ASEAN+3 approach for such things as financial cooperation, the exploration of the Mekong River Area, the establishment of an East Asian electronic communications network, a Europe–Asia railroad link, agricultural and food cooperation, and cooperation in human resources development, along with other initiatives. In the future, regional cooperation items can be designed and launched in the fields of energy, the environment, technology, scientific research, and other areas. A Pan-Asian communications cable network is on the way to being formed. If Pan-Asian railroads are built, the cost of Asian regional economic integration will be lower while the effects will be more substantial. Among plans for railway links, the ASEAN railroad from Kunming in China to Singapore will greatly advance subregional economic cooperation in the drainage area of the Mekong River, shortening the connection between the southwestern region of China and the Straits of Malacca by 2000 km to 4000 km.

At the present time, East Asian regional economic cooperation should stress the first and second mode while promoting multilateral cooperation under the auspices of the WTO. It should actively promote a free trade area but not be overanxious for quick results, being satisfied with step-by-step advancement.

4. Who Takes the Lead in Fostering East Asian Regional Economic Cooperation?

Promotion of regionalization of the East Asian economy not only means being clear and definite about the basic framework and modes of cooperation, but also solving the problem of which country will take the lead and host any institutions set up to maintain such regional frameworks. There are several possible options: 1) Japan; 2) China; 3) Japan, China, Korea; 4) Japan, China, Korea, one or two founding ASEAN members.

The first and the second options are not desirable. China does not have enough power and does not want to take the lead; Japan is powerful, but might not want to take the lead or might not be successful in this role. Once a country is the representative or the leader of a regional cooperative unit, its degree of freedom in dealing with nations beyond the region are reduced. In the case of Japan this would mean change to the country's current relations with the United States. Neither China nor Japan is taken with the idea of one country taking the lead alone, regardless of which country it might be.

The third option is desirable in that it would encourage active Korean participation. This option seems more likely to encourage Japan, Korea, and China to work together to organize and coordinate the process of East Asian economic integration. The idea is to put Japan, Korea, and China at the heart of any regional economic zone, in much the way European nations take turns in hosting and guiding further economic cooperation in the European Union.

The fourth option also has its strong points. It might encourage the formation of an East Asian regional economic community and its smooth working if one or two nations from ASEAN, with Singapore or Malaysia being the most likely choices, took the lead in fostering East Asian regional economic cooperation. The Singaporean government is active in furthering East Asian regional economic cooperation. At an informal ASEAN+3 conference held November 22–25, 1999, in Beijing, Singaporean Prime Minister Chok Tong Goh formally put forward the suggestion that an East Asian free trade area be formed, including Japan, Korea, and China. The Malaysian government is also enthusiastic about East Asian regional cooperation. If I were to choose, I would select the fourth option.

5. What Are the Ideological and Political Obstacles?

5.1 The Big Power Threat

One obstacle to East Asian regional economic cooperation stems from the notion of a "big power threat." Those who suggest that a country like China, so much larger in terms of population and economic potential than other nations in the region, is a threat have always been with us. In Japan, in particular, there are those who fear a resurgent China. Admiral Blair, in charge of U.S. forces in the Pacific region, recently expressed his opinion of the so-called China Threat, saying, "Most nations in the Asia-Pacific region have developed military forces for self-defense, with the exception of China and North Korea. China threatens Taiwan with the help of its guided missiles and relatively modern military. It maintains a military force for the purpose of aggression." More than 20 years since the country embarked on a process of reform and openness, China has become a nucleus for peace and stability in the Asia-Pacific region and the world at large. Fears of a "China Threat" are thus misplaced and must be abandoned.

Meanwhile, the so-called Japan Threat still hovers over parts of East Asia and exercises a strong influence. While it has a historical basis, it concerns modern-day problems as well. Japan spends more on its military than any other nation in the world except the United States. Despite a history of aggression and calls from some within Japan for the nation to take on a role as a major military power, the notion of a "Japan Threat" are as misplaced as the worries over a "China Threat." We must acknowledge that the Sino-Japanese relationship is the cornerstone of East Asian regional cooperation. Japan and China must work to constantly improve their relationship, and should aim for a shared commitment to cooperation. This is the only approach that offers long-term benefits for both the Chinese and Japanese people.

5.2 Merits and Demerits

One ideological obstacle to East Asian regional economic cooperation comes from consideration of economic interests. ASEAN nations are worried that Chinese goods may flood their markets after China's entry to the World Trade Organization (WTO). There are also some who have another worry. At present China already sets tariffs on some goods at considerably higher levels than do ASEAN countries. If China lowers its tariff again, more goods from ASEAN will enter China's market. This would increase China's trade deficit with the region.

More business opportunities will emerge for both China and ASEAN nations as the full effect of China's accession to the WTO is felt. As Stanley Fisher, vice chairman of the International Monetary Fund, pointed out in August 2001, "It does not seem that China is drawing anything away from other nations. Some will invest in China, but some will seek business chances in Thailand, Indonesia, or Malaysia. I believe that if one of you is a big economic power, the surrounding nations will not necessarily lag behind. They might gain from this neighbor, as it is a two-way relationship, involving imports as well as exports." (Agence France-Presse news wire from Singapore, August 31, 2001). Since the 1990s, Sino-ASEAN economic business cooperation has developed at a fast rate. Since 1998, Chinese imports from ASEAN have gone up sharply every year. In 1999 imports increased by 1%, in 2000 by 48.6%. In 2001, the volume of bilateral trade surpassed $40 billion for the first time in history. Recently, China has begun encouraging domestic enterprises to work actively to attract investment from overseas.

Some enterprises based in ASEAN countries, especially Singapore, Malaysia, and Thailand, have already entered the Chinese market. There will be more in the near future. At the same time, ASEAN might be the first place for Chinese enterprises to seek investment sources from abroad. The complementary nature of China and ASEAN will, it seems likely, proceed to a further stage.

5.3 Conflict

The foundations of East Asian regional cooperation are still fragile because of the historical and political problems in the region and elements of external interference. In East Asia, there are several latent crises, notably the unification of the Korean peninsula, the unification or independence of Taiwan, the conflict over sovereignty of several small island chains in the South China Sea, militarism and authoritarianism, terrorism, and other problems. Because of all of these problems, it is necessary to foster goodwill and a spirit of cooperation in East Asia.

East Asian nations should take an active attitude to promoting the unification of the Korean peninsula and forging consensus between Taiwan and China. Peace is the basis of the development of a civilized society and state sovereignty is something that cannot be above this goal. The South China Sea conflict should be solved while acknowledging Chinese claims and allowing mutual exploration and use. The solution to historical and political problems should be sought in a diplomatic context with the aim of avoiding conflict and confrontation.

6. What Are the Economic Obstacles?

6.1 Economic Differences

The differences in terms of economic development among the East Asian nations are relatively large. If we rank them according to Gross Domestic Product (GDP) per capita, Japan belongs to class A; Korea, Singapore, Hong Kong, and Taiwan belong to class B; China, the Philippines, Indonesia, and Thailand belong to class C; while Vietnam, Cambodia, and Laos are in class D. This difference is an obstacle to regional cooperation, for these countries have different policies towards tariffs and industrial protectionism because of their different levels of development, and therefore also different attitudes towards opening their markets.

The difference in industrial structure among the East Asian nations is, however, relatively small. Except for China and Japan, which have their own industrial systems, the industrial structure found in East Asian countries has a marked similarity. The industrial potential of the "four little dragons" and the "four tigers" is similar: their export products are mainly electronic and electrical goods, oil products, textiles, and the like. Despite this similarity, their mutual complementariness is also quite obvious. Mutual complementariness is the basis of regional cooperation. The cultivation of mutual complementariness, i.e., stressing the industrial distribution of the region, is a powerful motivation for developing regional cooperation.

Table 2. The development of Sino-Japanese trade, 1990–2000 ($100 million, %)

Year	Volume	Increase rate	Export	Increase rate	Import	Increase rate	Income and expenses
1990	129.3	-11.8	88.7	8.9	40.6	-37.8	48.2
1991	202.8	22.3	102.5	13.9	100.3	32.2	2.2
1992	235.8	25.1	116.9	14.4	136.8	36.3	-19.8
1993	390.3	53.8	157.8	35.1	232.5	69.9	-74.7
1994	478.9	22.7	215.7	36.7	263.2	13.2	-47.5
1995	574.6	17.9	284.6	31.9	290.1	10.2	-7.2
1996	600.6	4.5	308.7	8.4	291.8	0.6	16.9
1997	608.6	1.2	318.2	3.0	289.9	-0.6	28.3
1998	578.9	-4.8	296.6	-6.7	282.1	-2.7	14.9
1999	661.7	14.2	323.9	9.2	337.7	19.4	-13.7
2000	831.7	25.7	416.5	28.5	415.1	22.9	1.4

The statistics are based on information from China Customs

Source: 1990–1999: Chinese Ministry of Commerce (various issues), 2000: Customs General Administration of PRC (2000)

6.2 Trade Protectionism

Regional economic cooperation requires that all the nations in a given trade bloc open their markets. In recent years, East Asian countries have called for regional cooperation, yet at the same time trade protectionism is gaining ground. First, it must be noted that in recent years Sino-Japanese trade friction has intensified. Since 1997, the average Japanese import tariff on three kinds of agricultural products, including Chinese scallions, was raised from 3% to 6%, but later Japan announced high tariffs above these limits, e.g., the tariff on Chinese scallions was raised to 256%. On November 23, 2000, China began to impose anti-dumping duties on acrylic ester produced in Japan and imported into China. On March 22, 2000, the Japanese Ministry of Agriculture set a limit on imports of certain agricultural products from China. On April 23, Japan suddenly set a 200-day "limit" for imports of the three agricultural products mentioned above. On June 8, Japan announced a complete ban on imports of all poultry and poultry products from China. On the same day, China decided to impose special tariffs on cars, portable and vehicle-loaded wireless telephones, and air-conditioners imported from Japan. On June 21, China announced the imposition of a 100% special tariff effective from June 22 on the three Japanese products previously mentioned (Wu 2001).

Japan has been China's largest trading partner for eight years, since 1993, whereas China is Japan's second-largest trading partner. In 2000, Sino-Japanese trade volume reached $83.17 billion, an increase of 25.7% compared with the year before. In 1999, China's trade deficit with Japan was $1.37 billion, while in 2000, China's trade surplus with Japan was $0.14 billion. But according to Japanese statistics, Japan's trade deficit with China was $24.93 billion in the same year. The great statistical difference is mainly a result of the method used to compile Japanese statistics. Japanese statistics are based on the place of production. Imports from China include entrepôt trade via Hong Kong and Taiwan. This is not appropriate (Xu 2001a).

China and Japan are important trading partners for each other. It is unavoidable that problems will arise as bilateral trade increases, but increasing frequency of trade clashes should be avoided for fear of following the same road traveled in the United States–Japan trade war. It is necessary to avoid the adoption of discriminatory measures, such as setting limits, and it is also important to deal properly with problems in trade so as not to kindle new friction.

At the same time, Sino-Korean trade friction has begun to increase. Korea is China's third-largest trading partner. In 2000, the bilateral trade volume reached $34.5 billion, an increase of 37.8% over the year before when it was $25.04 billion. The rate of increase between Korea and China, Korea's largest trading partner, is higher than that in the trade between China with Japan, at 25.7%, or that between Korea and the United States, Korea's second-largest trading partner, at 21.2%. By the end of 2000, Korea was the fourth-largest source of foreign investment in China, coming only after the United States, Japan, and Singapore. The fast economic growth in the two countries not only provides a rich source for export production but also a large market for imports.

Table 3. The development of Sino-South Korean trade, 1988–2000 ($100 million)

Year	Total of import and export		Export to Korea		Import from Korea		Difference
	Value	Increase	Value	Increase	Value	Increase	Value
1988	2.9	—	0.9	—	2.0	—	-1.1
1989	8.9	214.0	4.7	437.9	4.2	114.7	0.5
1990	19.4	116.9	12.6	166.8	6.8	61.3	5.8
1991	32.5	67.0	21.8	72.9	10.7	55.8	11.1
1992	50.3	54.9	24.1	10.4	26.2	146.0	-2.2
1993	82.2	63.5	28.6	18.9	53.6	104.3	-25.0
1994	117.2	42.5	44.0	53.9	73.2	36.5	-29.2
1995	169.8	44.8	66.9	51.9	102.9	40.6	-36.0
1996	199.9	17.7	75.1	12.3	124.8	21.2	-49.7
1997	240.5	20.3	91.2	21.5	149.3	19.6	-58.1
1998	212.6	-11.6	62.7	-31.3	150.0	0.4	-87.2
1999	250.4	17.4	78.1	24.9	172.3	14.7	-94.2
2000	345.0	37.8	112.9	44.6	232.1	34.7	-119.2

Source: Customs General Administration of PRC (various issues)

China's trade deficit with Korea has increased considerably. In 1992, it was $0.22 billion, while in 2000 it reached $11.92 billion. Korea places stress on increasing exports to China, while restraining the amount of Chinese commodities entering the Korean market, which influences even the normal development of bilateral trade. By the end of 2000, total direct Korean investment in China had reached $10.03 billion. Considering the large Chinese trade deficit, Korean exports to China should not be looked at as capital but commodities. From 1988 to the end of 2000, the total Chinese trade deficit with Korea exceeded $50 billion (Table 3).

In June 2000, a Sino-Korean trade dispute caused much concern. Korea decided to impose a tariff of 315% on garlic imported from China, with the excuse that too much garlic was entering the Korean market. After several bilateral consultations, a memorandum on the Sino-Korean garlic trade was signed and the garlic problem was solved (Xu 2001b).

7. What Is the Significance of China's Economic Development?

At present, with the general decline of the world economy and the economies of East Asia, the continued rapid growth of the Chinese economy is of great importance for the development of East Asia in the following ways.

Table 4. Expansion and predictions of the commodity trade of China, 1998–2002 ($100 million)

	Import and Export		Export		Import		Volume of Trade
Year	Total	Increase (%)	Total	Increase (%)	Total	Increase (%)	Difference
1998	3239.5	-0.4	1837.1	0.5	1402.4	-1.5	434.7
1999	3606.3	11.3	1949.3	6.1	1657.2	18.2	292.3
2000	4743.1	31.5	2492.1	27.8	2251.0	35.8	241.1
2001. 1–9	3761.7	8.9	1947.9	6.9	1813.5	11.2	134.4
2001[a]	5030	6.1	2580	3.5	2450	8.8	130
2002[a]	5320	5.8	2675	3.7	2645	8.0	30

[a] Predicted value

Source: Group 2001

7.1 Creation of Market Requirements for Investment and Export

During the first three quarters of 2001, the total of Chinese imports and exports was $376.15 billion, an increase of 8.9% compared with the preceding year. Exports amounted to $194.79 billion, an increase of 6.9% and imports to $18.135 billion, an increase of 11.2%. The volume of Chinese exports to Japan and ASEAN fell, although both still increased in value by 10% and 7.3%, respectively. The annual total value of Chinese trade is estimated to be about $503 billion, representing an annual increase of about 6%. The export volume is about $258 billion, an increase of about 3.5%; the import volume about $245 billion, an increase of about 8.8%. In the first half of 2002, Chinese economic growth slowed, but it is likely to rise in the second half of the year. The rate of increase for the whole year will still be above 7%. In 2002, the total of goods trade is predicted to be $532 billion, an increase of about 5.8%. The rate of increase of exports will still be lower than that of imports at 3.7% compared to 8% (Table 4).

7.2 Increased Regional Financial Security and Resilience to Risk

After the outbreak of the East Asian financial crisis in 1997, the Chinese government provided aid within its powers and promised not to devalue the yuan, thus making a contribution to the stability of the regional financial order. Since then the Japanese yen has fallen markedly in value while the yuan retains its value.

7.3 A Powerful Economic Engine

In 2000, the total value of Chinese imports and exports reached $474.3 billion with regional trade in East Asia accounting for 51% of the total. In 2001, a similar pro-

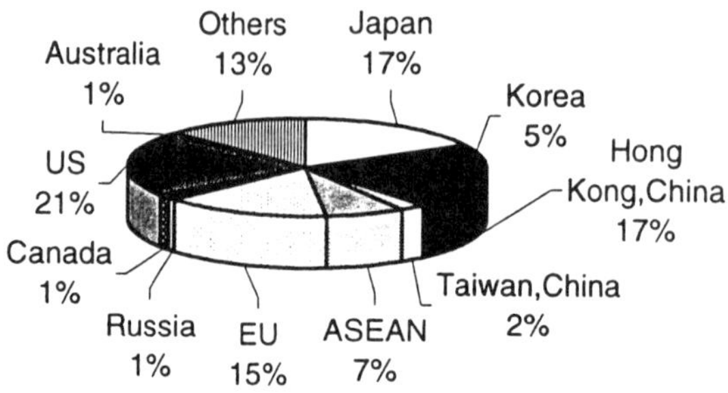

Fig. 1. Structure of the Chinese export market, January–September 2001. Source: Autumn Report 2001

portion was maintained (Fig. 1). Since entry to the WTO, China has provided a more open market, which means a rapid increase of exports as well as the possibility of more imports. Now many Chinese enterprises are investing to build factories in ASEAN countries and there is a tendency towards a continuous increase. In recent years, Sino-ASEAN trade has increased considerably. During the first ten months of 2000, the total of Chinese imports and exports with nine ASEAN countries (excluding Cambodia) reached $32 billion, an increase of 47.9%, in which the increase of exports was 45% and that of imports 50%. According to statistics from the ASEAN Secretariat, China has now become the seventh-largest ASEAN export market, after Japan, the United States, Hong Kong, Germany, Korea, and Taiwan (Customs Statistics 2000). China is a developing-economy power, and hopes for the East Asian economy overall now rest on the prospects for continued economic expansion in China.

8. How to Enhance Inter-governmental Coordination

8.1 Macroeconomic Policy Coordination

It is necessary to solve the problem of policy coordination with regard to the huge gap in East Asian economic development. A “bilateral–multilateral–regional” mode can be adopted, i.e., coordinating policies step-by-step in order to promote the construction of cooperation frameworks such as the East Asian Free Trade Area. Second, it is important to communicate and optimize the details of cooperative policies and measures accepted by a majority of East Asian nations. This primarily means selective governmental intervention including the provision of special item loans and discount interest loans for particular industries, maintaining low-interest deposit loans, fixing a maximum interest rate, increasing the profits of various enterprises, raising profit reservations, protecting domestic substitution of production to replace imports, establishing and financially supporting governmental banks, providing public investment for applied research, encouraging information exchange on the output of enterprises and industry, pursuing an import-substitution policy including encouragement of exports and foreign capital investment on favorable terms (Li 2001).

8.2 Strengthening Communication and Consultation

Government leaders and government departments should set up communication channels to form institutions for rapid response and cooperation.

8.3 A Trilateral Mediation Institution

In 1998, the domestic political situation in Cambodia became increasingly turbulent. In order to push forward reconciliation in Cambodia, ASEAN decided to form a coordination group of foreign ministers from Indonesia, Thailand, and the Philippines to go to Cambodia for mediation. The results were positive. At the end of 1999, the Prime Minister of Thailand proposed the establishment of a "trilateral mediation institution" to be used by ASEAN to deal with crises. At the 33rd ASEAN Foreign Ministers' Conference, held in 2000, those present decided to accept this suggestion as a means to deal with internal conflict or dispute. This institution should be enlarged to cover ASEAN+3 or even extended to cover the whole of Asia's economic and political life.

8.4 Cooperation in Politics and Security

Sino-Japanese cooperation is the key to East Asian political security. Generally speaking, the development of Sino-Japanese economic ties has been smooth, but resentments built up over history or the negative effect of domestic issues can create friction in this relationship. Sino-Japanese cooperation needs to be promoted from outside. The United States, Korea, and ASEAN can act to push forward Sino-Japanese cooperation. There is a degree of concern in Japan that Korea and China might unite to restrain Japan; while China worries that Japan and the United States might unite to restrain China. Thus, ASEAN is ideal as the leader in promoting Sino-Japanese cooperation. Malaysian Prime Minister Mahathir once proposed that an East Asia Economic Caucus (EAEC) be created, intending to push China and Japan into the same cooperative framework at the same time, but the United States was against this proposal. This shows that at the time the United States was not willing to promote any further development of Sino-Japanese cooperation. If Sino-Japanese cooperation is the basis of the ASEAN+3 regional cooperation framework, then a push by ASEAN is a powerful motivation for constructing an East Asian regional cooperation framework.

During the Cold War, China and ASEAN were suspicious of each other. Now the situation has changed. We are obliged to restrain confrontation, to enhance mutual trust, to establish true partnership with friendly neighbors, and develop mutual confidence. The problem of the South China Sea is an obstacle for China and some ASEAN nations preventing them from developing greater political security cooperation, but we need to solve this problem diplomatically according to international rules so as to lay another important basis for East Asian regional cooperation.

References

Autumn Report (2001) Autumn Report of 2001 on Chinese Foreign Trade Situation (in Chinese). Chinese Academy of International Trade and Economic Cooperation

Chen H (2001) Rely on self-decision. International Trade 11 (in Chinese). Chinese Academy of International Trade and Economic Cooperation

Customs General Administration of PRC (various issues) China's customs statistics. 1988–2000

Group of "Report on Chinese foreign trade situation" (2001) Negative influences that cannot be ignored. Trade Institution at Foreign Trade Ministry, Beijing. In: International Trade 11 (in Chinese)

Li T (2001) East Asian economy under globalization and China. The Journal of World Economy 8 (in Chinese). Institute of World Economics and Politics, Chinese Academy of Social Sciences

Wu D (2001) Collision of economic interests. International Trade 7 (in Chinese)

Xu W (2001a) Increase slows down. International Trade 3 (in Chinese)

Xu W (2001b) Look for balance. International Trade 5 (in Chinese)

Chinese Ministry of Commerce (various issues) Yearbook of Chinese foreign trade statistics, 1990–2000

7. Experience and Prospects of Financial Cooperation in ASEAN

Pasuk Phongpaichit and Chris Baker

1. Introduction

In December 2000, the U.S. National Intelligence Council published a report on *Global Trends 2015* which projected world "drivers and trends" as background for U.S. policy-makers to plan foreign, security, and military policies. The report paints a generally optimistic picture of world trends in the economy, resources, technology, politics and conflict, and expects the United States will face no major difficulty in managing the world over the next 15 years. However, at the very end, the report lists eight "significant discontinuities" that could "produce trends quite different from those presented in the body of the study." These eight include: economic collapse in the Middle East; "the formation of an international terrorist coalition"; another global epidemic on the scale of AIDS; an ethnic/religious conflict in a strategically sensitive area; a powerful anti-globalization movement; a China (People's Republic of China)–India–Russia pact against the United States; and the collapse of the Atlantic alliance. The last of these "significant discontinuities" reads:

> Major Asian countries establish an Asian Monetary Fund or less likely an Asian Trade Organization, undermining the IMF and WTO and the ability of the U.S. to exercise global economic leadership (National Intelligence Council 2000: 81).

It is likely that over the time since the issue of this report, the Asian Monetary Fund (AMF) issue has lost salience among American concerns, and it is certain that the terrorist issue has come to dominate since September 11, 2001. Even so, it is instructive to find the prospect of a successful AMF or ASEAN Free Trade Area (AFTA) listed as a threat to American world hegemony alongside international terrorism, AIDS, and an anti-U.S. pact by all the major nuclear powers.

This indicates clearly that the attempts by ASEAN to expand its role into economic and financial areas cannot be isolated from strategic concerns, the relations between ASEAN member-countries and outside powers, and especially the United States' conception of its role as the leading world power in both the military and economic realms.

This point dictates the plan for this chapter. While the focus of the chapter is on the debates and experiments over new financial measures in Asia since the 1997–

1998 crisis, this is preceded by a brief discussion of ASEAN's role as a security organization, and as the basis of a free trade area. Finally, these ASEAN financial debates and experiments are set into their international context of political and financial realities. We suggest that while the *substance* of financial cooperation as discussed (reserve pooling) may not yet be very significant, the *forms* of cooperation projected (networks of bilateral agreements extending over a wide area of Asia) may be more important as pointers to the future.

2. ASEAN's Origins as a Security Organization

ASEAN began life as a political organization to negotiate the internal conflicts that resulted from neighborly quarrels, and from the long history of outside intervention in the region during the colonial era and the Cold War.[1] It later developed the AFTA; and still later, began to discuss issues of financial cooperation. This sequence — security, trade, finance — also reflects the organization's continuing ranking of priorities.

The priority of security concerns dictated ASEAN's major initiative in the 1990s, namely, bringing within the organization the states omitted during the Cold War — Burma (now Myanmar), Vietnam, Laos, Cambodia — and hence completing the coverage of the Southeast Asian region. However, this expansion of the grouping increased its internal complexity in several ways. First, the major states of the original ASEAN (Indonesia, Malaysia, Thailand, the Philippines) shared a common commitment to development through a free-market economy with limited government planning, whereas the new additions had a history as planned socialist economies. Second, the variation in per capita income among the original major states was in the range of six times. The inclusion of the new states raised this factor to around 20 times.[2] These two reasons significantly complicated attempts to develop the economic aspects of ASEAN.

Third, the expansion of the grouping brought in new problems over marine rights, and over cross-border flows of contraband, drugs, people, arms, disease, ideas, and political activism. These latter problems were particularly acute between Sumatra and Malaysia, and on the Thai–Burma border. The issue arose as to whether ASEAN was the proper forum to address such problems. Since many of these cross-border flows (arms, drugs, political activism) were clearly related to political arrangements, this issue challenged the past convention that ASEAN should not interfere in the internal politics of its member states. The debate on this problem complicated the process of absorbing the new members, and diverted attention away from other issues in the late 1990s.

In addition, the political crisis in Indonesia weakened ASEAN in various ways. Indonesia had been the organization's original host and largest member, and hence the *de facto* leader. While Indonesia's political troubles distracted the country from this role, the leadership effectively was in abeyance. Besides, the Indonesian crisis also increased the problems of cross-border flows of people and arms, and led to fears of a trend of political unrest and potential "Balkanization" across the region.

Finally, the attacks of September 11, 2001, raised the issue of militant Islam in the region, and made it more likely that the United States would intervene in the region with potentially disruptive consequences. These problems have concentrated ASEAN's attention on its priority area of security, and distracted attention from other areas.

3. ASEAN as a Forum for Economic Cooperation

From its early days, ASEAN was projected to take on an economic role. The original 1967 declaration spoke of economic, social, and cultural cooperation. But initially, economic cooperation was valued as a means to achieve greater political cooperation. Also, economic cooperation was conceived within the framework of the state-led development planning prevalent in the 1960s and 1970s. Planners allocated major schemes of state investment-led development to different members of the grouping in order to achieve economies of scale for projects that were too large for a single country. However, despite a large investment in research and negotiation to launch these projects, the results were meager — partly because of political discontinuities in the member states, partly because of inter-country rivalries, but mostly because of the transition away from state-led to private-led development thinking between the 1970s and the 1990s.

The idea of trade cooperation emerged into prominence around 1990 in reaction to events elsewhere in the world. The European Community made the transition to the European Union. The United States began the negotiations that resulted in the North America Free Trade Agreement (NAFTA) in 1994. For many it appeared that the world was quickly becoming divided into regional blocs (Nattapong 2001). After several meetings on the topic in the early 1990s, ASEAN leaders agreed on the goal of achieving some kind of economic union in the future, but conceded that this goal was remote because of inter-country differences and the lack of experience in economic cooperation. As an interim measure, they agreed to move towards an AFTA by progressive rounds of customs rate reductions. The original program targeted tariffs no higher than 5% by 2008, but had many exclusions (especially agricultural products). After ASEAN was expanded from six to ten members in the mid-1990s, the goal was restated as zero tariffs, and schedules drawn up for the four newer members extending to 2018 (Ariff 2000: 46–48).

At the onset of the financial crisis, ASEAN leaders anticipated that the crisis would provoke a lapse into protectionism, and countered with a "Bold Resolution" to *accelerate* the schedules for customs reduction by one year (from 2003 to 2002). While governments acceded to this idea in the first instance, many subsequently negotiated exceptions and exclusions for pet projects, specific products, and priority sectors (Malaysia for automobiles, the Philippines for petrochemicals, Indonesia for sugar). In January 2002 ASEAN formally abandoned the accelerated schedule as only two countries had achieved the targeted minimum tariff of 5%.[3]

Even without these difficulties, trade integration progressed slowly. In reality, the ASEAN countries are more competitive than complementary in the realm of trade. All have pursued a similar strategy of developing export markets in the advanced world. Intra-ASEAN trade as a proportion of the grouping's total trade grew only from 18% in 1990 to 23% in 1996, then lapsed to 21% by 1998. Given that this was a period of increasing overall trade, this represented some achievement. However, compared to the EU (63%) and NAFTA (51%), the proportion of intra-group trade was small (Nattapong 2001: 66–68).

Besides, the open pattern of ASEAN countries' trade meant that AFTA from the beginning faced political opposition. External trading partners were concerned about being excluded. Australia and New Zealand in particular believed they needed to be connected to an Asian grouping. The United States also moved to protect a small but potentially important part of the "Pacific" economy, which in the early 1990s was widely projected to become the fastest growing part of the world economy in the twenty-first century. As a result, the formation of AFTA provoked the formation of other cross-cutting groupings. The most significant of these was the Asia Pacific Economic forum (APEC), which included the United States, Australia, and a miscellany of other countries which had an interest in trading with Southeast Asia.

In addition, the conclusion of the Uruguay round of trade talks and the transition from the General Agreement on Trade and Tariffs (GATT) to the World Trade Organization (WTO) raised the issue of the role of regional free trade projects within the context of an overarching WTO framework for global trade liberalization.

In sum, by the time ASEAN took an interest in financial cooperation in the late 1990s, the grouping was already involved in considerable soul-searching over its role and future. The expansion of the grouping, the resulting issue of cross-border flows, the implications of the Indonesian political crisis, and the global consequences of September 11 tended to focus ASEAN on its primary security role. At the same time, the indifferent results from trade cooperation, the implicit conflict between AFTA and the WTO, and the appearance of competing regional groupings discouraged progress towards economic cooperation. Singapore's foreign minister admitted that ASEAN had become perceived "as ineffective and a sunset organization" (Tay 2000: v). Several enquiries into the future economic role of the grouping, conducted at the end of the millennium, concluded bravely that some forum of cooperation was better than nothing at all (e.g., Tay 2000; Abidin 2001). But these optimistic assessments have to confront two key issues. First, how far can economic cooperation progress without greater political cooperation? NAFTA is held together by the domination of the United States. The EU was created by a shared desire to move beyond the murderous nationalisms of the twentieth century. What equivalent power or sentiment can underlie regional economic cooperation in Southeast Asia?

Second, in what way does ASEAN make sense as an economic grouping if most of the members' economic fortunes are tied up with outside players, and if the most important of these outside players (the United States) is antagonistic to any effective economic grouping?[4]

4. Moving Towards Financial Cooperation

Before the Asian financial crisis of 1997–1998, Southeast and East Asian governments showed little interest in regional financial cooperation. The idea of creating a regional monetary fund had been mooted at the time of the establishment of the Asian Development Bank (ADB) in 1966, when proponents saw an International Monetary Fund (IMF) equivalent in Asia complementing the activities of the ADB in the same way as the IMF complemented the activities of the World Bank. But the idea failed to materialize. At the time, most Southeast and East Asian nations had dollar-pegged currencies and closed capital accounts. They were not too concerned about international financial instability. These attitudes changed in the 1997–1998 crisis for the following reasons.

First, from the perspective of countries affected by a liquidity crisis either directly (Thailand, Korea (Republic of Korea), Indonesia, Malaysia) or indirectly (Japan, the Philippines, Singapore, China, and others), the absence of a suitable lender of last resort was a great drawback. The inadequacy of the IMF rescue plans drove home to these countries the need for a regional financial arrangement suitable to regional needs. The amounts available to these Asian countries as emergency aid under the IMF quota system were very low. As a result, funds had to be collected on an ad hoc basis by a kind of "whip round" among sympathetic states. This was clumsy and politically fractious. Thailand in particular was disappointed that the United States refused to commit any bilateral financial assistance, even though Thailand considered the United States to be an old ally going back to the Cold War period. This incident led other Asian countries to doubt the American commitment to stabilize the regional economy under crisis.

Second, the programs imposed on Thailand and Indonesia (and to some extent Korea) as conditions for the IMF assistance proved incapable of preventing much deeper crises than anybody had expected, and a wave of contagion spread across the region and the world. The IMF deployed much the same rescue package that had been applied earlier in Latin American countries, even though the Asian problem of private debt was fundamentally different from the Latin American countries' problem of public debt. The results were severe capital flight and a sharp contraction of GDP, with dire social and economic consequences (Pasuk and Baker 2000).

Third, the IMF and its United States patrons took the opportunity to attribute the crisis to a faulty "Asian model" of development, to demand the lowering of barriers to the entry of foreign capital, to create opportunities for buying up banking and other assets at "fire-sale" prices, and to impose legal and administrative reforms. Inevitably, these moves were interpreted as attempts to gain a greater role for American business in a region from which the United States had partially withdrawn in the 1970s, and where it now regretted the prominence of Japan.

Fourth, the crisis exposed the vulnerability of the foreign exchange regimes of most Asian countries, which were pegged to the U.S. dollar in one way or other before the crisis. This raised the question of the need to diversify beyond the dollar into other currencies, particularly the strong currencies of the region such as the yen or yuan (Katada 2001).

Given this environment, Japan saw an opportunity to take a leadership role in enhancing regional cooperation to establish a regional financial framework. Two areas of Japan's concerns were 1) plans for emergency funding facilities ranging from an AMF to currency swap arrangements; and 2) promotion of increased use of the yen, as part of diversifying currency use beyond the dollar.

For Japan, the proposal for an AMF was defensive geopolitics of self-preservation in the sense that a regional monetary framework in Asia would reduce the effort and cost of maintaining Southeast Asia as a prosperous place for Japanese firms to do business, and would help Japan insulate its economy from international financial instability (Katada 2001). For ASEAN, increased usage of the yen, in line with the importance of Japan as a trade and investment partner, would prevent the distortions and fluctuations introduced by changes in the yen-dollar parity (Rajan and Bird 2002).[5]

Most ASEAN countries responded positively to Japan's plan for an AMF, but were cautious over the increased use of the yen. An AMF would, they perceived, offer them a more effective lender of last resort in future financial crises. But the institutionalization of this project was complicated by the geopolitics in the international arena and in the region.

5. The Asian Monetary Fund Debacle

The move towards financial cooperation within ASEAN during the crisis surfaced *not* in ASEAN itself, but in Japan.

The idea of an AMF had been discussed among officials of the Japanese Ministry of Finance in the mid-1990s. The 1997 proposal for an AMF independent of the United States was championed by Eisuke Sakakibara, Japan's Vice Minister for International Finance. In July 1997, Sakakibara spearheaded the effort to raise funds for Thailand beyond its IMF quota. Most of these funds came from countries in the region. Sakakibara concluded from this experience: "At that time, we thought it was a good opportunity for Asian countries to recognize that the Asian currency crisis was our own problem, and that we could strengthen regional cooperation within Asia" (Sakakibara 1999). In August 1997, Sakakibara floated the idea of an AMF — a fund of $100 billion to act as a regional lender of last resort — at a meeting in Tokyo of the countries that had contributed to the rescue package for Thailand. He repeated the idea in informal meetings with other financial agencies and central banks in the region in August and September of 1997. Finally the initiative was made official by Japan at the G-7 and IMF meeting in Hong Kong in September 1997.

The United States reacted with strong opposition (Altbach 1997; Acharya 1999; Higgott 2000). Sakakibara recounts that U.S. deputy treasury secretary Lawrence H. Summers rang him at home after the G-7/IMF meeting and stated angrily: "I thought you were my friend" (Sakakibara 1999). American policy-makers feared that an independent regional monetary fund would duplicate the IMF, reduce the IMF's role in the region, and increase the possibility of moral hazard due to softer conditionality if the AMF were managed by Japan independent of the IMF. Stanley Fischer called the AMF "a threat to the authority and effectiveness of the IMF itself."

The Chinese response to Japan's initiative was one of silence. This was interpreted as not lending support. China's participation, however, was key to the success of a regional fund because China is the region's second-largest holder of foreign exchange reserves. China's silence may have reflected its cautious stance towards the United States as China was at the time negotiating its entrance to the WTO. The Chinese may also have been concerned about a new regional institution led by Japan.

Once the United States objected strongly and China remained silent, neither Japan nor the ASEAN countries wished to move forward with the scheme. For all the ASEAN countries, their good relations with the United States were as important as their relations with Japan. China's non-cooperation further added to the complications (Katada 2001; Amyx 2001).

At this stage the crisis had not become contagious. But when the crisis spread to Indonesia in October 1997, and the IMF's harsh conditionalities led to the collapse of Indonesia's banking system, apprehension about the IMF's effectiveness intensified. This encouraged 14 countries representing the Asia-Pacific region to convene a meeting in Manila in November 1997 to discuss a framework for strengthening Asian regional cooperation for stability. This gathering included the United States, Canada, Australia, and New Zealand. At the meeting the countries agreed that deputy finance ministers and central bank deputies of their countries should meet twice a year to discuss international finance and the conduct of monetary surveillance in the region. Subsequently, ASEAN set up a Surveillance Co-ordinating Unit to collect and share financial information that might help predict and prevent a crisis. The project was supported by the ADB which also established a unit and website to make some of the information available beyond the public sector (Rajan 2001a: 132–133). The Manila meeting also proposed programs of technical support to strengthen the financial sectors and market management in member countries. Further, the countries concluded a Cooperative Financing Arrangement (CFA), an agreement to help one another in the event of any future crisis. Essentially this was a loose institutionalization of the role that Japan had played to persuade other countries to contribute to the bailout packages for Thailand and Indonesia through networks of bilateral agreements. This bilateral assistance was designed to be implemented *after* an IMF agreement was in place and only if IMF resources were found to be inadequate. This so-called Manila Framework brought the IMF back into the picture.

Through 1998 and 1999, Japan increased the support offered to crisis-hit Asian countries, particularly through the Miyazawa Initiative launched in October 1998. After the crisis spread to Russia (summer 1998), the long term credit management (LTCM) collapse (September 1998), and serious problems in Brazil, the United States became more appreciative of Japan's efforts to re-establish financial stability and cushion the impact of the crisis in the Asian region. In addition, possibly to quieten the financial panic, both the United States and Japan seemed to become more concerned about scotching any impression that they were in serious conflict over plans to stabilize Asia. In late 1998 and early 1999, the United States and Japan worked together within the G-7 framework to restore regional stability and reform the international financial architecture. The G-7 endorsed the creation of a new Contingent Credit Line (CCL) within the IMF as a mechanism of crisis prevention. Financial authorities in G-7 countries held the first meeting of the Financial Stability Forum, with the aim of making the international system less vulnerable by strengthening regulatory and supervisory measures on highly leveraged hedge funds, offshore markets, and short-term capital flows.

6. From the Asian Monetary Fund to the Chiang Mai Initiative

Through 1999, as criticism of the IMF increased, and as proposals for a large-scale revision of the international financial architecture crumbled into a few piecemeal adjustments, Japan restated that the vision of Asian monetary cooperation was still alive,[6] and some ASEAN countries (particularly Thailand and Malaysia) encouraged Japan to assert its leadership. The revised scheme that Japan helped to evolve over 1998–1999 differed from the original AMF proposal in three crucial ways.

First, the idea of establishing a new *institution* — with all the practical difficulties and political implications — was temporarily shelved in favor of a simpler *framework of cooperation.*

Second, the discussion on techniques for stabilization began to focus on currency swap arrangements. By 1999, it was clear that countries that had strong reserves were in a better position to evade the sort of financial panic that overcame Asia in 1997–1998. Moving from fixed to floating exchange rates might remove some of the distortion that caused crises such as that which afflicted the baht, but it did not remove the rationale for holding strong reserves to deter the kind of financial attacks that happen when a crisis becomes contagious (Rajan and Bird 2002; Rajan 2002). In his review of the 1997 crisis, for example, Stanley Fischer of the IMF emphasized the importance of reserves (Fischer 2001). Many Asian countries over the next two years made a priority of rebuilding or increasing their levels of international reserves. By extension, the idea of *pooling* reserves through currency swap arrangements became attractive as a first step towards regional financial cooperation. In March 1999, Japan took the first step in this direction by assigning part of the funds available under the Miyazawa Initiative to set up the Asian Currency Crisis Support Facility at the ADB, and concluding currency swap arrangements with Korea ($5 billion) and Malaysia ($2.5 billion).

A third difference was that the scale of cooperation was expanded beyond ASEAN (or Japan plus ASEAN). ASEAN members in fact already had an agreement for currency swaps originally concluded in the 1970s and reconfirmed in 1997. But the scale of this arrangement was small ($200 million) compared to the large amounts required to combat the 1997–1998 crisis. Besides, the spread of the crisis to adjacent countries had made it clear that cooperation between equally weak neighbors was unlikely to be effective. For reasons of both scale and politics, any financial cooperation within Asia needed to incorporate the region's strongest countries.

As a result, Japan's initiative on currency swaps was discussed not so much within ASEAN as within larger groupings such as the APEC symposium in July 1999, and within a new grouping (ASEAN+3), which assumed importance because of this issue of financial cooperation. In 1997, ASEAN had held a meeting jointly with China, Japan, and Korea on the fringes of the 30th anniversary ASEAN summit. This meeting set up a scheme of biennial meetings of finance officials. The currency swap proposal was discussed at the meeting of deputy finance ministers of this grouping in Manila in November 1999. The meeting issued a formal statement on financial cooperation. The currency swap scheme was then announced during the meeting of the grouping's finance ministers during the ADB annual conference held in Chiang Mai in May 2000.

While the grouping was dubbed rather clumsily 'ASEAN+3,' which appeared to give ASEAN a leading role, in reality the importance of the grouping was in the "+3." China, Japan, and Korea were the largest economies in the region with the strongest reserves (Table 1). This grouping recognized the fact that financial cooperation within ASEAN alone made no sense. Despite its clumsy name, ASEAN+3 was really the germ of a pan-Southeast–East Asian grouping of great importance. Interviewed at the Chiang Mai meeting, Sakakibara said: "When you sink, we sink and vice versa. So it's about time Japan looks to ASEAN countries, Korea and China."[7]

The Chiang Mai Initiative (CMI) had three parts: the existing swap arrangement between ASEAN countries would be increased in value; Japan, Korea, and China would conclude swap agreements among themselves; and these three would then negotiate a total of 15 separate bilateral swap agreements with ASEAN members.

The third difference between AMF and CMI was that the new arrangement incorporated the IMF, and thus overcame the concerns of both the United States and China. China warmly welcomed the scheme, which gave China a leading role on an equal footing with Japan. The United States was initially of two minds. The Ameri-

Table 1. Foreign exchange reserves of Asian countries, 2000

Country	Foreign exchange reserves 2000 $ billion	Percent of GDP
Japan	286.9	7.0
Korea	96.1	21.0
China	168.3	18.4
Hong Kong	107.6	65.8
Taiwan	106.7	36.4
Thailand	31.9	26.0
Indonesia	27.5	18.5
Malaysia	30.6	32.6
Philippines	14.5	19.1
Singapore	80.4	82.2

Source: International Institute of Finance estimates (Rajan and Bird 2002)

can representative at the Chiang Mai meeting cautiously welcomed the scheme, but added that there was no substitute for internal financial restructuring. He then heavily criticized the ADB, including a warning "not to duplicate the work of other institutions," and ending with a threat that the U.S. might reconsider its funding for ADB (Truman 2000).

But Japan moved rapidly to overcome American objections. At Chiang Mai, Sakakibara insisted that the CMI was a step towards his concept of an AMF, but accepted that "the fund's role could be restricted to the provision of liquidity with conditions for private sector participation and surveillance, while the macropolicy recommendation function could be handled by the IMF" (*The Nation* [Bangkok], May 6, 2000). Moreover, a few months later, Sakakibara was replaced as vice minister for finance by Haruhiko Kuroda, who had earlier been seconded by the Japanese Ministry of Finance to work at the IMF, and was known to be more amenable to working within IMF guidelines (Amyx 2001). Japan impressed upon ASEAN members that the IMF would have to be involved in the scheme. In fact, the Japanese Ministry of Finance had always been concerned about monitoring the financial workings of other states. At the outset of the crises in Thailand, Indonesia, and Korea, Japan had refused requests for direct support, and directed these countries to the IMF, for precisely the reason that it doubted its ability to monitor these countries' economies. Japan, China, and Korea — the countries with large reserves which could expect to be lenders under the CMI scheme — all felt they needed the IMF experience in surveillance (Amyx 2001).

When the details of the CMI scheme were announced in November 2000, 90% of the funding was available only to countries operating under an IMF program. Malaysia had earlier objected strongly to any IMF involvement, and it seems likely that the remaining 10% was arranged as a sop to Malaysian sentiment. Other ASEAN members publicly welcomed the IMF role.

In March 2001, ASEAN finance ministers announced that they had progressed the Chiang Mai Initiative by upgrading the intra-ASEAN swap agreement from $200 million to $1 billion, with additional provisions for members to draw funds against holdings of hard currency instruments such as U.S. treasury bills.

Japan concluded swap agreements with Thailand ($3 billion), Korea ($2 billion), and Malaysia ($1 billion), and began negotiations with the Philippines and other countries (Ministry of Finance 2001). In May 2001, ASEAN+3 established study groups to investigate surveillance mechanisms. In late 2001, Thailand stated that it was also negotiating a swap agreement with China.

Japan continued to insist that the network of swap agreements represented progress towards a more ambitious framework of monetary cooperation in the future. Critics pointed to the limited scale and slow progress of the project. Japan also remained interested in expanding the international usage of the yen, but other Asian countries remained lukewarm. During the crisis, most countries found that their use of the dollar increased because of the enhanced importance of the United States as an export market and source of investment. However, against the background of the EU's progress towards a common currency, the idea of some future monetary union remained attractive. A feasibility study for a common ASEAN currency was inserted in ASEAN's "Hanoi Plan of Action" adopted in 1999. The joint Asia–Europe meeting (ASEM) in Kobe in January 2001 initiated a research project on monetary cooperation in Asia, using European expertise and experience. At the meeting, the IMF's Horst Koehler foresaw "greater monetary integration" in Asia's future (quoted in Rajan and Bird 2002). But any substantial move towards monetary cooperation is perceived as remote.

7. The Revival of Trade Cooperation

Over 2000–2001, the threat of financial crisis receded, while the prospect of a trade recession increased with the downturn in the United States and then the shock of the events of September 11, 2001. The focus of discussions on economic cooperation moved from finance to trade. However, these new discussions reflected two innovations that had first surfaced during the attempts to achieve financial cooperation. First, there was no central plan for cooperation, but rather a network of bilateral and multilateral agreements. Second, these agreements reflected an enlarged and flexible definition of the region for cooperation. By late 2001, the list of bilateral and multilateral free trade agreements under negotiation included Japan–Singapore; Japan–Korea; Japan–Korea–China; Korea–Chile; Korea–ASEAN; Korea–Japan–China–ASEAN; China–ASEAN; Singapore–New Zealand; and ASEAN–Australia–New Zealand (Ariff 2000; Salong 2001). At the end of the year, a plan was announced to create an ASEAN–China free trade area "within ten years."

At the APEC meeting in Shanghai in November 2001, financial cooperation was significantly downplayed. Thailand invited participants to review experience of the 1997 crisis, but only Hong Kong and the Philippines attended the meeting. Thailand also floated the idea of extending the Chiang Mai swap arrangement from ASEAN to APEC, but nobody responded to the proposal. Instead, the Shanghai meeting concentrated on trade cooperation. The meeting formally restated the APEC resolution on trade liberalization taken seven years earlier. It also implicitly blessed the trend towards achieving liberalization not through a centralized plan but through a network of bilateral and multilateral agreements. It suggested that the ultimate goal of liberalization would best be achieved through a "pathfinder system" under which "those who could run faster should run faster and ought not to be held back by those who choose not to run or do so at a snail's pace" (quoted in Rajan 2001b).

8. Conclusion and Prospects for the Future

Let us now summarize the major points of our argument and examine their implications for the prospect of financial cooperation in the future.

Financial cooperation is one form of international cooperation. It cannot be isolated from other aspects. It takes place within the broad framework of international relations. It is subject to the pressures of international powers, and constrained by the complexities of local political realities.

ASEAN countries had little interest in financial cooperation until the 1990s, when most of the member countries liberalized their capital account and become vulnerable to international financial instability. At this time however, ASEAN as a grouping was distracted by the security concerns that were the grouping's initial reason-for-being. Optimism about financial cooperation was also dulled by the rather indifferent past record of economic cooperation. The discussion of financial cooperation within ASEAN could never be separated from the broader context of the region's relations with the United States, China, and Japan.

The impact of the 1997–1998 crisis focused interest on financial cooperation, but the nature of the crisis indicated that such cooperation *within ASEAN* was unlikely to be effective. The crisis emphasized the vulnerability of countries with small economies (in world terms) to international financial flows, and the likelihood that a crisis in one country would rapidly spread to its neighbors. Hence cooperation among a group of adjacent countries of equal financial weakness was unlikely to be effective.

The plans for financial cooperation that emerged in 1997–1998 did not come from ASEAN itself or the ASEAN nations. Indeed, throughout this period, ASEAN as an institution played no effective role in the financial sphere. The lead role in constructing financial cooperation was taken by Japan — from its initial efforts in organizing financial support for Thailand in July 1997, through the doomed AMF proposal in September, the Manila Framework in November, and the extension of the Miyazawa scheme to currency swap arrangements in 1999. The Japanese role in promoting financial cooperation was a product of an overall Japanese economic policy in the Asian region — namely to develop the region's prosperity and to develop Japan's role as a regional leader. The initial plans were torpedoed by the United States and China, which for different reasons were opposed to Japanese ambitions.

The afflicted countries concentrated on defending themselves by administrative, banking, legal, and monetary reforms. They adopted various measures to protect their capital accounts including capital controls and currency restrictions. As part of the same thinking, as the crisis receded, most made a priority of building up their international reserves. The recognition that international reserves still served as a bulwark against financial disaster, even in a world of floating exchange rates, created the opportunity for cooperation among countries through currency swap arrangements. Again it was Japan that crafted the idea into a regional project.

This time Japan overcame the objections of the United States and China by bringing in the IMF as the scheme's administrator, and by giving China an equal role. The new scheme was significant in two important ways. First, it helped to bring into existence a new regional grouping (ASEAN+3) which had the potential to become a pan-East–Southeast Asian arena of cooperation.

The United States might have some concerns about the political implications of such a grouping. Indeed, ASEAN+3 is remarkably similar to the East Asia Economic Caucus that Mahathir championed in the early 1990s, and which the United States and other Western states strongly opposed (Tay 2000). However, owing to the crisis the United States was forced to reassess its own independent capability within Asia, and to acknowledge the local roles of both China and Japan in managing the crisis.

Second, the swap arrangement was organized not as a centrally administered scheme, but as a network of bilateral pacts. In parallel, new proposals for trade cooperation that emerged over 2000–2001 took a similar form. This new format reflects political realities: Asian countries are too diverse to move at a single pace; external economic relations are more important than internal ones; centralized schemes and organizations attract the political antagonism of excluded participants and hegemonic international powers.

The currency swap scheme is arguably too small to be a realistic bulwark against future financial crises. But the experience of creating the scheme has given rise to a new grouping and to a new technique of organization which perhaps better reflect the political realities of constructing economic cooperation in the region

References

Abidin MZ (2001) ASEAN and its interregional economic links. In: Mya Than (Ed) ASEAN beyond the regional crisis: challenges and initiatives. Institute of Southeast Asian Studies, Singapore

Acharya A (1999) Nationalism, institutionalism and the Asian economic crisis. Contemporary Southeast Asia 21:1 (April)

Altbach E (1997) The Asian Monetary Fund proposal: a case study of Japanese regional leadership. JEI Report 47 (19 December)

Amyx J (2001) U.S.–Japan financial cooperation and competition in Asia: From the Asian Monetary Fund proposal to the Chiang Mai Initiative. Paper for the conference on "Beyond bilateralism: U.S.-Japanese cooperation and competition in Asia", Kona, Hawaii, 28 June – 1 July

Ariff M (2000) Trade, investment and interdependence. In: Tay SSC, Estanislao J and Soesastro H (Eds) A new ASEAN in a new millennium. Centre for Strategic and International Studies, Jakarta and Institute of Southeast Asian Studies, Singapore

Fischer S (2001) Opening remarks. International reserves: policy issues forum. IMF/World Bank, Washington DC (28 April)

Higgott R (2000) The international relations of the Asian economic crisis: a study in the politics of resentment. In: Robison R, Beeson M, Jayasuriya K, Kim H (Eds) Politics and markets in the wake of the Asian crisis. Routledge, London New York

Katada SN (2001) Japan and Asian monetary regionalization: Cultivating a new regional leadership after the Asian financial crisis. Geopolitics 6.

Ministry of Finance, Japan (2001) Progress of the Chiang Mai Initiative. http://www.mof.go.jp/english/if/ekaigi008a.htm

National Intelligence Council (2000) Global trends 2015: a dialogue about the future with non-government experts. National Intelligence Council, Washington DC (December)

Nattapong T (2001) ASEAN Free Trade Area: progress and challenges. In: Mya Than (Ed) ASEAN beyond the regional crisis: challenges and initiatives. Institute of Southeast Asian Studies, Singapore

Pasuk Phongpaichit, Baker C (2000) Thailand's crisis. Silkworm Books, Chiang Mai

Rajan RS (2001a) Financial and macroeconomic cooperation in ASEAN: issues and policy initiatives. In: Mya Than (Ed) ASEAN beyond the regional crisis: Challenges and initiatives. Institute of Southeast Aian Studies, Singapore

Rajan RS (2001b) The Shanghai summit: Hope in global despair. http://www.economics.adelaide.edu.au/rrajan/briefs.html

Rajan RS (2002) Safeguarding against capital account crises: unilateral, regional and multilateral options for East Asia. In: De Brouwer G (Ed) Regional financial arrangements in East Asia. Routledge, London New York

Rajan RS, Bird G (2002) The evolving Asian financial architecture. Princeton essays in international economics. Princeton University, Princeton NJ

Sakakibara E (1999) Thai crisis played part in AMF idea. *Yomiuri Shimbun* newspaper [*Daily Yomiuri*] 26 November

Salong I (2001) Regionalism in Asia and the Pacific. Asian Development Bank, Manila

Tay SSC (2000) ASEAN and East Asia: A new regionalism? In: Tay SSC, Estanislao J, Soesastro H (Eds) A new ASEAN in a new millennium. Centre for Strategic and International Studies, Jakarta and Institute of Southeast Asian Studies, Singapore

Truman EM (2000) Statement to the Asian Development Bank. http://www.usa.or.th/news/press/2000/nrot054.htm (8 May)

Wanandi J (2000) ASEAN's past and the challenges ahead: aspects of politics and security. In: Tay SSC, Estanislao J, Soesastro H (Eds) A new ASEAN in a new millennium. Centre for Strategic and International Studies, Jakarta and Institute of Southeast Asian Studies, Singapore

World Bank (2001) World development report 2000/2001. Oxford University Press, New York

Notes

1 ASEAN was founded in 1967. The immediate background was the confrontation between Indonesia and Malaysia, and the initial concern was the impact of the Vietnam War on the region (Wanandi 2000). The initial members were Indonesia, Thailand, Malaysia, the Philippines, and Singapore, with Brunei joining later. In 1995, the original six were expanded to ten with the inclusion of Cambodia, Laos, Burma, and Vietnam.

2 World Bank estimates (Table 1) of 1999 GNP per capita in U.S. $: Malaysia 3,400; Thailand 1,996; the Philippines 1,020; Indonesia 580; Vietnam 370; Laos 280; Cambodia 260 (World Bank 2001: Table 1). Burma cannot be estimated but is often reckoned to be below $200.

3 *The Nation* [Bangkok], 21 January 2002. The two countries were Brunei and Singapore.

4 The millennial debates on ASEAN's future included other issues which added to the complication, particularly environmental issues thrown up by the "haze" from Indonesia's forest fires; the welfare implications of regional cooperation; the need to cooperate against cyber-crime; and the importance of democracy (Tay 2000; Abidin 2001).

5 In particular, incorporating the yen into "baskets" used for currency adjustment would have avoided the overvaluation that affected the Thai baht and other currencies when the value of the dollar rose in the mid-1990s.

6 "If the IMF can be likened to a major hospital caring for the world as a whole, then we should consider supplementing it with the establishment of an Asian Monetary Fund to serve as a 'family physician' to provide care at a more intimate level. We have reached the stage at which we should take a multilevel approach in the field of finance as well, responding both globally and locally." Prime Minister's Commission on "Japan's Goals in the 21st Century" (statement on January 18, 2000; cited in Amyx 2001).

7 Interviw by Suthichai Yoon in *The Nation* [Bangkok], May 15, 2000.

8. Towards a New Framework of Regional Integration in East Asia

Young-Ho Kim

1. The Necessity of Establishing FTAs in East Asia

A new era of regional integration has begun in East Asia. The ASEAN Free Trade Area (AFTA) will be virtually realized as of 2002; a free trade agreement (FTA) between the People's Republic of China (China) and ASEAN has been endorsed; a pan-Chinese FTA among China, Taiwan, Hong Kong, and Macao is under discussion; a Japan–Singapore Economic Partnership Agreement (JSEPA) has been concluded between Singapore and Japan; negotiations on an FTA between Japan and ASEAN are now in progress; an FTA joining all the countries in East Asia was discussed at the most recent ASEAN+3 summit; and discussions to form an FTA between Japan and Korea (Republic of Korea), or among Korea, Japan and China, have begun. Discussions on FTAs of various forms have, in other words, gained considerable momentum in East Asia.

There have been 162 regional integration agreements set up so far, of which about 90 were concluded between 1996 and 2001. The world is riding the crest of FTAs, and now East Asia is joining the trend. As to regional economic integration, East Asia is considered the least developed area in the world and, in particular, Northeast Asia is the worst example. An FTA is the first stage of economic integration, bringing about many economic effects such as creation of trade, transformation in trade patterns, transformation of investment patterns, expansion of markets, promotion of competition, and reform of domestic economic institutions.

However, in the case of East Asia, I can add two additional effects which are much more important than those found in other cases. First, there is the "escape" (or isolation-free) effect that will enable Northeast Asia to escape from its relatively isolated situation, resulting from the fact that most of the countries in the world with the exception of those in Northeast Asia are involved in FTAs. Because about 70% of international trade is conducted under FTAs, with the proportion rapidly increasing, countries that are not linked to FTAs are likely to find themselves in increasingly disadvantageous positions. For example, if an FTA between Mexico and Europe becomes effective, tariff rates in Europe will be reduced from 20% to 3.3%, and in 2003 they will be cut to zero. Considering the fact that a 20% average tariff rate continues to be imposed on Japanese and Korean exports, their price competitiveness will surely be weakened.

Second, an FTA is necessary to neutralize or absorb any damage caused by globalization. (A currency swap agreement among East Asian countries is considered a good example of a common cooperative response to global financial challenges.) It also works as a countermeasure to globalization, at the regional level. Considering the recent experience of economic crisis that swept East Asia, it is an urgent task to have an FTA in the region. From this point of view, an FTA in East Asia is not a matter of choice but of necessity, not an object of consideration but of determination.

2. Existing Constraints

Despite the fact that an FTA is imperative in East Asia, especially in Northeast Asia, the actual situation for achieving these aims is not good. There are some explanations why the region has seen the slowest movement toward the signing of agreements.

First, there are still strong feelings of nationalism in Northeast Asia, which act as a barrier to regional economic integration. The fact that China and Southeast Asia show greater progress in the area of free trade in spite of the relative underdevelopment of their economies and civil society indicates that the prevalence of nationalism rather than the development of a market economy and civil society is the key factor in forging FTAs. The competition between China and Japan to conclude FTAs with ASEAN may be interpreted as nationalistic antagonism between the countries.

Another problem, one that is deeply related to the issue of nationalism, is the legacy of historical distrust and relatively high levels of armament. The United States is deeply involved in this matter. Therefore, Northeast Asian countries are less dependant on neighboring countries than on the United States for security. Japan's friendly relationship with America is one that Korea and Taiwan try to imitate. The Chinese economy is highly dependent on America's market, technology, and capital, and so is the economy of North Korea (Democratic People's Republic of Korea). The same thing happens in Northeast Asian politics. Tokyo–Beijing and Seoul–Pyongyang relations inevitably involve Washington, as do the Tokyo–Seoul and Tokyo–Pyongyang relationships. In these circumstances, how can regional economic integration in Northeast Asia move forward? French intellectual Jacques Attali pointed out that "Europe's penitence for history creates the regional integration." In the case of East Asia, however, penitence for the sins of the past has not been done, preventing the region from achieving regional economic integration. So far, East Asia has successfully overcome poverty and political oppression. Now it needs to be free of the ghosts of history. One of the conditions for economic integration in Northeast Asia is freedom from history. The relatively faster progress toward establishment of FTAs in Southeast Asia is partly due to the fact that these countries are not as confined by historical problems as are Northeast Asian countries.

Third, there is a big gap in income among East Asian countries. Citizens in European countries and the North American Free Trade Area (NAFTA) countries have five-digit incomes, while those in Southeast Asian countries have four-digit incomes and those in African countries a three-digit income. However, Northeast Asian countries have three income strata: three-digit, four-digit, and five-digit. A vertical international division of labor is seen among countries in the region and there is a wide gap in competitive power among nations in the area. Hence, the disproportionate balance of trade among nations has not been addressed.

This demonstrates the poor conditions for the establishment of FTAs in this region. Additionally, the power of the agricultural lobby in both Japan and Korea means that there is little will in these countries for liberation of trade in agricultural products. It is worth noting that the agreement between Japan and Singapore is the Economic Partnership Agreement (EPA), not an FTA, with the former excluding the agricultural sector. The FTA agreement between Korea and Chile cannot advance toward agreement because there is no political will to pacify the farmers' objections to liberalization in this area. Besides, unlike what we find in the European Union, Japan seems to give little consideration to the developed countries' "early harvest" policy implementation in East Asia. This makes a big difference, as seen in the fact that the Chinese side initiated the implementation of an early harvest policy in the FTA agreement between China and ASEAN.

This is likely to create tension, due to the gap between objective necessities and actual conditions. Because of continuous tension, any FTA might be difficult to bring into existence but could then develop strength quickly, as described by A. Gerschenkron [1962].

3. New Framework in East Asia

In the case of the European Union, there has been a shift from national to supranational authority. The three layers of power consist of supranational, state, and regional authority. These three layers offset one another through the subsidiary principle [Tsoukalis 1991]. The higher-level power is confined to the area where the lower powers are unable to act. However, with neo-functionalism, the benefits of regional integration will gradually diffuse. As a result, in the long run, the growth of both top-level power (at the supranational level) and lower-level power (local government), middle-level power (the nation-state) is controlled. This evolved in the case of the EU from the European Economic Community (EEC) to the European Community (EC) to the EU. The pattern has been described by Balassa [1961], who outlines the shift from customs union to a common market and then on to economic and monetary union, setting the stage for complete economic integration and political union.

However, this was possible because of the maturity of civil society in Western Europe. The maturity of civil society has evolved as follows: penitence for history; civil state power; flexible balance between the three levels of power; the development of a consumer-based economy; and the fostering of competition. However, in East Asia, where there is neither a strong history of civil society or a mature con-

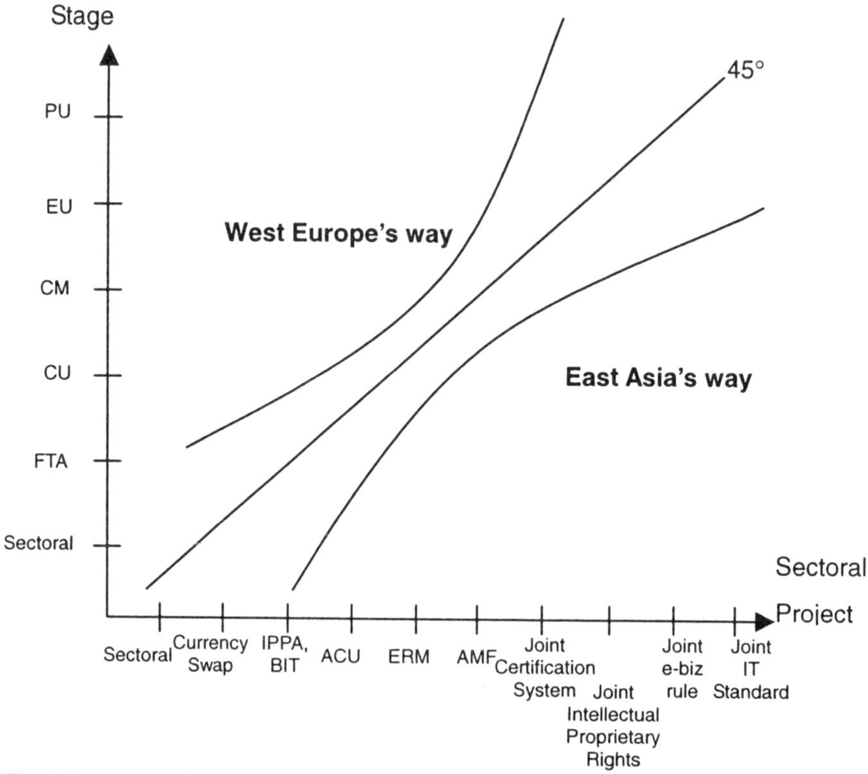

Fig. 1. Two ways of regional integration. Source: Kim Y-H, unpublished data. Note: FTA = Free Trade Area; CU = Custom Union; CM = Common Market; EU = Economic Union; PU = Perfect Union; IPPA = Investment Promotion and Protection Agreement; BIT = Bilateral Investment Treaty; ACU = Asian Currency Unit; ERM = Exchange Rate Mechanism; AMF = Asian Monetary Fund

sumer-oriented economy, a realistic regional integration framework different from that of Western Europe is required.

In East Asia, especially in the case of Northeast Asia, intra-state power tends to coalesce rather than transforming into supranational frameworks, meaning that ad hoc agreements between individual nations are required. In addition, there is a considerable possibility that a framework for local governments to act as the subordinate power can be created. The macro frameworks selected as necessary in intrastate power and regions within the state will create a double framework. In short, integration will proceed at the regional level within a larger macro-level framework, forming a dual structure with non-integrated parts.

In Western Europe, the main causes of international disputes of the past, including disputes over coal- and steel-producing areas have been sublimated by the European Coal and Steel Community (ECSC) in an example of cooperative management at the European level. Similar managerial frameworks in East Asia may, however, be used to evade issues of importance.

The process of industrialization generated the middle-class income group and the civil society, while economic integration is based on the premise of a mature civil society already in place. This means that the lack of a mature civil society in East Asia presents real challenges for the establishment of regional economic cooperation frameworks, but flexibility and a willingness to adapt to the conditions of the region will bring the benefits of such frameworks within reach.

In Fig. 1, the vertical axis represents the steps toward economic integration as detailed by Balassa. These include FTAs, customs union, common market, economic union, and perfect union. The horizontal axis shows various forms of economic cooperation among nations in East Asia. For example, the currency swap set out in the Chiang Mai Agreement makes it possible to secure international liquidity in exchange for national currency when foreign reserves run short. The upper limit of the currency swap between Korea and Japan is set at $7 billion. The Asian Currency Unit (ACU) is the Asian version of the European Currency Unit (ECU) in the EU, aiming at creating a new common currency in East Asia for transactions involving goods and services among member countries instead of the U.S. dollar.

4. IT-FTA

As pointed out above, there is a strong possibility in East Asia that regional economic cooperation frameworks will develop quickly after taking some time to come into existence. This would be the result of piecemeal initiatives of the type represented by the horizontal lines in Fig. 1, rather than regional economic integration of the type indicated by the vertical lines in the figure. East Asia now faces the challenges and opportunities of the digital age. As the digital economy has just begun, almost all countries, regardless of whether they are developed, share the same opportunity to compete against one another, all beginning from the same starting point. Japan, China, Singapore, Taiwan, and Korea have all set out to jump-start developments in this area. The new technology frontier is where we can expect the big spurt to occur in East Asian economic integration. As the European economic union started with the European Coal and Steel Community, the Northeast Asian economic union could start with cooperation in the information technology (IT) area. There are many ways in which IT might be used to foster economic integration, including mutual certification systems, IT technology standards, unified intellectual property rights, common e-commerce standards, an e-business network in East Asia, the establishment of a dispute settlement system, and the establishment of an e-trading system.

We look forward to the creation of a digital FTA in East Asia [KIEP/IDE 2000]. While we can characterize the Japan–Singapore FTA as less than complete because it excludes the agricultural sector, an IT-FTA might be characterized as an FTA plus. There is a saying that "e-business is business," meaning that e-business will eventually incorporate all forms of business. In the future, nearly all business in East Asia will develop into e-business, with IT industries highly integrated. Countries in East Asia should not wait for the development of the IT industry to begin building an IT-FTA, but should initiate a common strategy for developing such frameworks by constructing common infrastructure and designing common promotion schedules for an IT-FTA.

For this, we need to link the IT revolution to the FTA revolution, which is essential to enhancing the competitiveness of the IT industry in East Asia. At the same time, we should allow free movement of IT specialists across borders in East Asia and examine the possibility of establishing a common labor market for the IT industry. To bring such ideas into existence, we need to issue a common certificate for IT experts. In Korea, gold cards have been issued to foreign IT experts to enable them to enter Korea easily. Because East Asian countries do not generally have permanent residency as in the United States, the gold card is issued instead of a green card. The gold card system could be expanded to cover all East Asian countries. In addition, East Asian countries could build up a common IT training center. In East Asia, it would not be an easy task to set up means by which general laborers could move freely across borders, but it would be possible to limit free movement to IT experts. In this regard, we can think of the possibility of building up an IT common market and an FTA at the same time.

At the same time, a common oil market in East Asia could be initiated. It could change the oil market from a seller's market into a buyer's market. With the introduction of e-business practices in the oil market, we can also develop this into a kind of oil FTA or East Asian Oil Common Market.

5. Korea–Japan FTA or Korea–China–Japan FTA?

The question of a Korea–Japan FTA or a Korea–China–Japan FTA is a complicated one. Since 1998, according to arrangements between the Korean and Japanese governments, joint research on a possible FTA involving the two countries has been carried out by the Korea Institute for International Economic Policy (KIEP) in Korea and the Institute of Developing Economies (IDE) in Japan as well as by a South Korea–Japan business forum. These discussions have reached the stage of submitting an official petition recommending an FTA to the two governments. Addition-

Table 1. Effects of abolition of tariffs between Korea and Japan

		IDE	KIEP
Japan	Welfare standard (%)	0.03	0.146
	GDP (%)	0.00	0.04
	Trade balance with Japan (hundred million $)	38.85	0.90
	International trade balance (hundred million $)	54.79	—
Korea	Welfare standard (%)	0.34	-0.19
	GDP (%)	0.06	-0.07
	Trade balance with Japan (hundred million $)	-38.85	-60.90
	International trade balance (hundred million $)	-2.5	-15.43

Source: KIEP/IDE [2000]

Table 2. Effects of a Korea–Japan FTA by industry

Major industrial categories	Effects on production, trade, and investment in Japan and Korea
Textiles/clothing	Abolition of high tariffs imposed on certain products would help increase exports to Japan. Japanese companies would counter by producing more high-end, fashionable items. This might increase their exports to Korea.
Chemicalproducts	The two countries are closely matched in terms of technical ability and competitive strength. Abolition of tariffs that remain on certain products would increase mutual imports/exports. Both countries have surplus facilities, so cooperation in facility disposal and division of labor regarding the production of competitive items is possible. Division of labor exists between the two countries in synthetic textile materials. There is a possibility that European and U.S. corporations may penetrate the market.
Metals	No direct influence of an FTA is expected as both countries abolished tariffs on steel at the Uruguay Round. There will be more cooperation in disposing of surplus facilities and increased division of labor regarding production (due to Japan's higher costs) through strategic collaboration between Korean and Japanese corporations. As a result, mutual imports/exports should increase.
Electricalmachinery	With Korean companies catching up with their Japanese counterparts, exports of household electric appliances to Japan have increased. However, this is partly due to tariffs and to the system of categorizing countries from which it imported goods that have protected these companies. An FTA may intensify competition, but collaboration with Japanese corporations has created the potential for technology transfers and divisions of labor/production.
Generalmachinery	Japan has the competitive advantage. When Korea abolished its 8% tariff, Japan's export surplus increased. Korea may collaborate with Japanese corporations for the transfer of technology; divisions of labor/production are possible by taking advantage of Korea's lower costs.
Transportation Machinery	Both Japan and Korea actively export passenger cars to third countries, but import and export very few between themselves. With liberalization in Korea (lifting of the 8% tariff on passenger cars and the 13% tariff on components), exports from Japan should increase, although exports of low-priced items from Korea to Japan should increase as well. Japanese companies may advance into the parts sector and replace imports. Exports of technology may also increase.
Other manufactured goods	With the abolition of high tariffs, imports from Korea should increase, although there may be restrictions in terms of quality. Taking advantage of cost-competitiveness in furniture and other products, Korea may make inroads into the Japanese market. Japan should increase exports of miscellaneous famous-brand goods to Korea
Transportservices	Mutual imports and exports are likely to show an increase, although because of its price advantage, Korea will continue to register a surplus in exports.
Travelservices	Mutual exchanges should increase following expedited visa procedures and joint use of air and marine services. Owing to its low commodity prices, however, Korea should continue to register a substantial surplus in exports.
Other services	Mutual imports and exports are likely to show an increase in other profit-making businesses and various other services. Korea should continue to dominate in construction services, and Japan in patent-rights usage fees and financial services.

Source: KIEP/IDE [2000]

ally, with the final draft of the Korea–Japan Bilateral Investment Treaty (BIT), being approved in December 22, 2001[1], it can be said that the first stage of an FTA arrangement involving the two countries is already underway. It is time for both countries to take further action.

Among the effects of a Korea–Japan FTA, expected tariff reductions would not be particularly marked because Japan's average tariff rate is 2%–3%, while Korea's tariff rate averages 7%–8%. However, Japan applies a tariff acceleration rule in which the rate increases in stages on products thought to compete with domestic producers in certain industries. In the case of processed foodstuffs the rate is 35.1%, for semi-processed goods it is 36.1%, and a 64.5% tariff is levied on finished goods. Since some products thought to offer competition to domestic producers are those that would be most affected by an FTA, manufacturers of these products are expected to resist the establishment of an FTA.

The effects of a Korea–Japan FTA and tariff abolition are summarized in the following tables [Kim 2002].

However, the problem of non-tariff barriers is much more serious than that of tariff barriers, as the former are applied in a wide range of areas and in an arbitrary way, distorting trade practices to a large extent. World Trade Organization (WTO) and United Nations Conference on Trade and Development (UNCTAD) criteria are used to regulate non-tariff barriers, but Japan imposes quantity restrictions as a non-tariff barrier, using such techniques as selective inspections, medical inspections, distribution practices, standards, and certification. In this regard, there is a fundamental difference between Japan and other countries. If these kinds of non-tariff barriers are removed as part of an FTA, the effect will be considerable. Neither the IDE nor the KIEP examined the subject of the abolition of non-tariff barriers, however.

The biggest stumbling blocks to a Korea–Japan FTA are Japan's agricultural sector and Korea's auto parts and components industry. Based on a mutual understanding of these obstacles, we should seek out gradual solutions. The greatest benefits of a Korea–Japan FTA would be the development of a more mature civil society and development of a stronger IT industry in both countries.

Assisted by a mature civil society and the cooperation of non-governmental organizations in both countries, international attention has been successfully drawn to the problem of the so-called comfort women (women forced to provide sexual services to Japanese military personnel during World War II in military occupied areas)

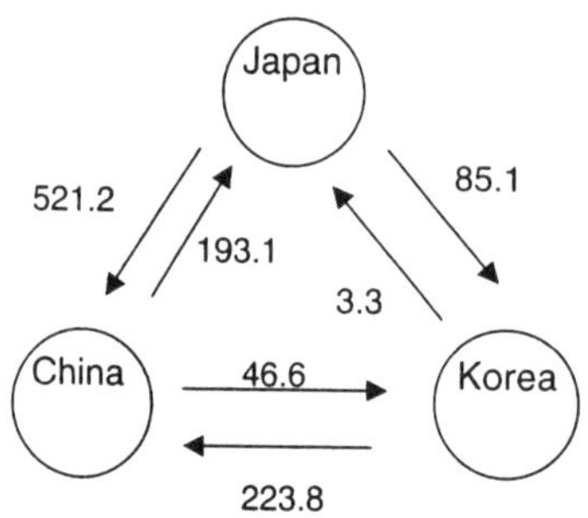

Fig. 2. The export accretion effect of a Korea–China–Japan FTA. Source: Kim Y-H, unpublished data

and has frustrated past attempts for the official approval of revanchist history textbooks in Japan. The power of this society should now be used to foster the establishment of an FTA between Korea and Japan.

The effect of a Korea–Japan–China FTA would be much more extensive than that of a Korea–Japan FTA. However, a Korea–Japan–China FTA has both political and agricultural barriers. The former are related to security issues among the three countries. The latter are associated with strong resistance from farmers in Korea and Japan as the price competitiveness of agricultural goods in these countries is considerably lower than that of China .

6. Establishment of the East Asia FTA Promotion Committee

FTAs in East Asia have begun to show a competitive side because of the AFTA that was promoted by ASEAN, followed by FTAs such as the Korea–Japan FTA, the China–ASEAN FTA, and Japan's efforts to conclude an ASEAN–Japan FTA. This could possibly turn into a very complicated situation, with such arrangements as a China–ASEAN FTA; a so-called pan-China FTA that would include Hong Kong, Macao, and Taiwan, along with the mainland; and an FTA with members such as Japan, Korea, and other Asian countries competing against one another.

In this situation, I believe the promotion of competitive FTAs needs to be reexamined. It seems problematic because it would turn FTAs into a tool of national competition in East Asia. One forum for discussion incorporating the majority of the countries of East Asia is ASEAN+3, which includes the ASEAN nations plus Japan, Korea, and China. It would be beneficial if an FTA for all of East Asia were negotiated through this forum. An FTA should be set up within a framework for common welfare, developing specialization, mutual supplementation, and the encouragement of constructive competition.

To achieve this goal it will be necessary to set up an FTA promotion council with all the East Asian countries represented. This is all the more urgent when we consider the reality that most of the countries in East Asia are having trouble mustering the political capital necessary to form consensus about the need for FTAs. Even in Korea, an FTA between Korea and Chile that has been discussed is strongly opposed by domestic farmers. This demonstrates the necessity for setting up an East Asia FTA promotion council. If strong support is not garnered from business, academia, the press, and civil society, and if representatives of these groups do not participate in such a council, the idea of an FTA will in the end fail.

It is important to stress that the financial sector tends to be distinct from the trade sector, functioning as though it were independent. In East Asia, most countries are now experiencing trade surpluses, and the volume of intra-regional trade is increasing, accounting for about 50% of total trade volume. In contrast, the integration of the financial sector in the region is very limited, with a small proportion of surplus money circulated within the region. The high savings in the region are not directly invested in intra-regional projects, but flow into Wall Street. Money originating in East Asia but managed by Wall Street mutual funds then flows back into the region, giving U.S. firms considerable control of East Asian capital markets and influencing trade and investment in the region.

East Asian economic integration has shown some progress in terms of trade. Regional cooperation in the financial sector is still at a low level, however, a factor that often distorts trade flows. This means that East Asian economic integration should be promoted not only in the areas of trade and investment, but also in the financial sector. In this regard, currency swap agreements among East Asian countries arranged under the auspices of the Chiang Mai Agreement are an important step forward. Formulas such as the ACU, aimed at decreasing dependence on the U.S. dollar for intra-regional trade, the Asian Monetary Fund as a regional equivalent to the global IMF, an Asia bond market to trade bonds denominated in East Asian currencies, and the Northeast Asian Development Bank (NEADB) to pursue both development and peace in the region, are all worth noting. The advancement of cooperation and integration in the real economic sector in East Asia demands a still higher level of cooperation and integration in the financial sector, which will in turn consolidate cooperation and integration in the area of trade. It is very important to maximize the feedback effect between trade and finance in working toward East Asian economic integration.

References

Balassa B (1961) The Theory of Economic Integration. Richard D. Irwin, Inc; Homewood, Ilinois

Bergsten CF (1997) Open regionalism. Institute for International Economics (IIE) Working Paper 97-3, Washington DC

Bhagwati J, Panagariya A (1996) The Economics of preferential trade agreements. American Enterprise Institute, Washington DC

Cheng I-K (2001) How to cope with the expansion of FTAs? Korea Institute for International Economic Policy, Seoul, Korea

Gerschenkron A (1962) Economic backwardness in historical perspective: a book of essays. Belknap Press of Harvard University Press, Cambridge

International Monetary Fund (2000) Direction of trade statistics yearbook 2000. IMF, Washington DC

KIEP/IDE (2000) Toward the Korea–Japan FTA: assessments and prospects. Proceedings of the joint international symposium of the Korea Institute for International Economic Policy and the Institute of Developing Economies. KIEP/IDE, Seoul and Tokyo

Kim Y-H (2002) Toward a common house of East Asia. Rengo-Soken joint symposium proceedings, report 161. Rengo-Soken, Tokyo

Krueger AO (1999) Are preferential trading agreements trade-liberalizing or protectionist? Journal of Economic Perspectives 13:4 (Fall)

Munakata N (2001) Evolution of Japan's policy toward economic integration. CNAPS Working Paper, Brookings Institute, Washington DC

Tsoukalis L (1991) The new European economy: the politics and economics of integration. Oxford University Press, Oxford

United Nations (2000) Bilateral investment treaties, 1959–1999. UN, New York and Geneva
World Trade Organization (2000) Mapping of regional trade agreements. WTO Committee on Regional Trade Agreements, Geneva

Notes

[1] This BIT became effective in January 2003.

Subject Index